Ceramic Bead Jewelry

30 Fired & Inspired Projects

Jennifer Heynen

LARK BOOKS

A Division of Sterling Publishing Co., Inc.

New York / London

Senior Editor
Suzanne J.E. Tourtillott

Editor
Larry Shea

Art Director
Stacey Budge

Photographers
Steve Mann
Stewart O'Shields

Cover Designer
Cindy LaBreacht

Library of Congress Cataloging-in-Publication Data

Heynen, Jennifer.
  Ceramic bead jewelry : 30 fired & inspired projects / Jennifer Heynen. --
1st ed.
       p. cm.
  Includes index.
  ISBN-13: 978-1-60059-142-6 (hc-plc with jacket : alk. paper)
  ISBN-10: 1-60059-142-6 (hc-plc with jacket : alk. paper)
  1. Ceramic jewelry. 2. Beadwork. I. Title.
  TT920.H49 2008
  745.594'2--dc22

                                                              2007046536

10 9 8 7 6 5 4 3 2 1

First Edition

Published by Lark Books, A Division of
Sterling Publishing Co., Inc.
387 Park Avenue South, New York, NY 10016

Distributed in Canada by Sterling Publishing,
c/o Canadian Manda Group, 165 Dufferin Street
Toronto, Ontario, Canada M6K 3H6

Distributed in the United Kingdom by GMC Distribution Services,
Castle Place, 166 High Street, Lewes, East Sussex, England BN7 1XU

Distributed in Australia by Capricorn Link (Australia) Pty Ltd.,
P.O. Box 704, Windsor, NSW 2756 Australia

If you have questions or comments about this book, please contact:
Lark Books
67 Broadway
Asheville, NC 28801
828-253-0467

Manufactured in China

ISBN 13: 978-1-60059-142-6
ISBN 10: 1-60059-142-6

For information about custom editions, special sales, premium and corporate
purchases, please contact Sterling Special Sales Department at 800-805-5489
or specialsales@sterlingpub.com.

Contents

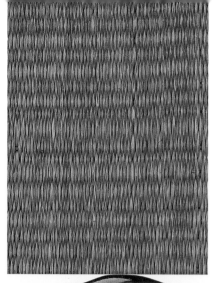

introduction

A wonderful teacher I had in high school used to tell me, "Clay is the way." It turned out to be true: I fell in love with the material immediately. You can move and shape it any way you want. You can cut it, roll it, or join it. You can grab it or stab it, push it or pull it, stamp it or smooth it, until it becomes exactly what you had envisioned. Then the piece is fired in the kiln and frozen in time.

For the first ten years of my love affair with clay, I made only tiles and pottery. Then I decided to try my hand at using clay to create beads. Unable to find any books on making ceramic beads, I set out to teach myself how on my own. After much trial and error—all self-taught artists understand that failure is a lesson learned, not a disappointment—I finally developed a method of making ceramic beads.

The remarkable variety—in shape, texture, color, and style—and incredible beauty of ceramic beads just knocked me out. But what really kept me making more (and more, and more) ceramic beads was the way you can use them to create fabulous jewelry. As you'll see in this book, ceramic beads can be arranged in a colorful strand on a bracelet, serve as the dazzling centerpiece of a necklace or ring, dangle invitingly from a pair of earrings, and much, much more.

Besides the wonderful things you can do with them, what's really great about ceramic beads is that anyone can make them. If you can roll clay into a ball, you've got the basic skills to begin making ceramic beads. I can't count all the beads my own three- and five-year-old kids have made. The art of it isn't in the technical expertise, but in the individual vision. In other words, it's not how you make them, it's what you make. With practice, you can even master complicated painting or intricate carving.

This book shows you everything you need to know to start making beads and creating eye-catching jewelry from them. The first few chapters introduce you to the clay, the tools, and the basic techniques.

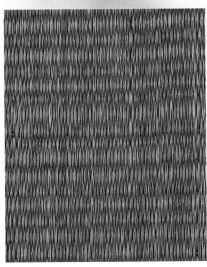

You'll learn how to work with the clay, shape it, decorate it, glaze it, and fire it. One thing you'll discover is that clay is an imperfect medium. Fingerprints often remain on the surface, as do other marks that show the piece was made by hand and with care. The possibilities for surface decoration are endless. You can, for example, delicately paint ceramic beads with soft watercolor-like glazes or with crusty raku glazes that require you to dunk the whole bead into flammable material like sawdust. With clay, the possibilities are infinite and the fun never stops.

Another advantage of ceramic beads you'll learn about is the small workspace they require. Starting out, you can set up on your kitchen table or even on a card table. The kiln is the only tool that can be expensive, but even if you don't have one, you can still make your beads. Call a local ceramics studio or a paint-your-own-pottery studio. Many of these places will agree to fire your work for a small fee. This is a great way to try ceramic bead making without the financial commitment.

The introductory chapters conclude with some basic jewelry-making techniques, and then the truly fun part of the book begins: the 30 fabulous jewelry projects. The projects start with easy-to-make jewelry (like the Cute Button Earrings) and grow progressively more involved (like the Heart Box pendant). Along the way, you'll get to experiment with techniques like mold-making, slip trailing, majolica underglazes, decals, and working with metal clay, just to name a few.

So get some clay and jump right in. Once you master one technique and create one dazzling piece of jewelry, another one is just a page turn away. As you work your way through the projects, I hope you discover, as I did, that "clay is the way."

CHAPTER ONE

basic tools
and materials

To get started making ceramic beads, you'll need at least some of the basic tools listed in the tool kit at right. It's a good-sized list, but don't worry—all that you absolutely need to get started is some clay and something to pierce a hole. Most of the tools listed here are inexpensive, and you might already have many of them hiding around your house.

Once you jump into making beads more fully, you'll be better able to decide what tools you really want. This chapter lists all of the tools used in the book, along with a brief description of each. First, though, we'll take a look at the basic materials—clay and glazes—those tools will be used to work with.

Choosing a Clay Body and Compatible Glazes

Ceramic clays and glazes can be grouped by the temperature you fire them to. I like working with low-fire clays and glazes because of their wide variety of colors and applications. The projects in this book all focus on low-fire clay and low-fire glaze applications, which are sturdy and can be watertight.

In ceramics, porcelain and high-fire stonewares require the hottest temperatures. You can fire high-fire clays with added elements such as wood, soda ash, or salt. These elements vaporize and create a glaze or surface covering. High-fire clays are normally fired in the range of cone 6–10.

Earthenware clays, on the other hand, are fired in the temperature range of cone 04–06, around 2000°F (1093°C). Raku and other low-fire glazes are compatible with these low-fire clays. You can use a variety of colored underglazes and overglazes formulated for low-fire, slips, and stains.

Ceramic Tool Kit

Bead racks (for the kiln)
Brushes (for glazes)
Cutters (cookie and donut)
Extruders
Hemostats
Kiln
Kiln stilts
Metal bucket (with sawdust, for raku)
Needle tools
Nichrome wires (for firings)
Pliers: flat-nose, needle-nose, and round-nose
Raku tongs
Reamers
Rolling pin
Ruler
Skewers
Slip trailers
Sponges
Stamps
Stands
Straws
Wire cutters
Wire tools
Wood slats

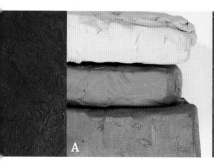

▷ *Test tiles in different colors with different glazes*

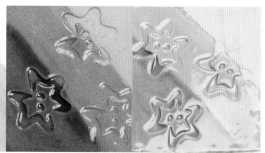

Low-fire glazes provide a greater intensity of color. If you were to fire these same colorants to high-fire, many would burn out or become muted. Low-fire clays can also be used in luster firings.

Another advantage of working with low-fire clays is that you can fire beads and other small items in just about any electric kiln. Small test kilns (also called tabletop kilns), annealing kilns, and metal clay kilns will all work. Make sure you check your manual to see that the temperature will reach cone 04–06. Cone 06 is 1828°F (998°C).

Clays come in a wide variety of colors, from pure whites and buffs to browns and reds (photo A). The temperatures at which they reach maturity vary. Play around with different colors because glazes look different depending on what clay color is underneath.

For most of the projects in the book, I used a low-fire white body, but you can use either red or white clay. Just make sure you clean your tools and fabric work surface thoroughly when switching, or the other clay color will show through your glazes.

What Does That Cone Number Mean?

In ceramics, a "cone" is a specified combination of firing temperature and applied heat. (The word "cone" also refers to actual cones used in the firing process. When you purchase these cones, they will come with a chart of relevant cone numbers and temperatures.) It may seem odd, but the lowest temperatures are found in cone 022, and temperature numbers go up as the cone number goes down up to cone 01. The temperatures then continue to rise as the cone numbers go from 1 up to 14.

You can think of this as similar to what happens with very cold winter temperatures: When the temperature goes below zero, higher numbers are colder; when it's above zero, higher numbers mean it's warmer. Or you can decide to not even try to understand this unusual system, and just look up the correct numbers on the chart. Either way, don't sweat it.

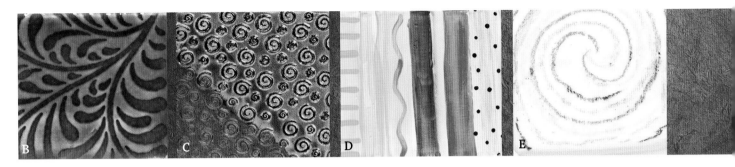

Glazes

You'll need low-fire glazes for the projects later in the book. Refer to each set of instructions for specific information. Here is an overview of the types of glazes and colors compatible with low-fire clay bodies. Any ceramic supply store will stock a wide variety of glazes.

Overglazes

Overglazes seal and protect your beads. Overglaze is basically crushed glass suspended in water. When the kiln heats up, the glass melts and flows together. Overglazes can be clear—useful for painting over underglazes—or they might have colorants in them. Colored overglazes sometimes break on the surface of a textured bead, giving a great effect. When two overglazes overlap on a bead, it usually creates a third glaze color (photos B and C).

Underglazes

Underglazes are colorants without the gloss. You can paint them on beads either on bisque or green, and you can thin them with water to create a watercolor effect or else use them full strength for bold color. You'll achieve better detail with an underglaze, along with a richer color and shine, if you paint a clear overglaze over it later (photo D).

Chalks, Stamps, and Pencils

Chalks, stamps, and pencils are all variations of underglazes that provide different effects. If you use them, you can still add an overglaze for gloss if you desire (photo E).

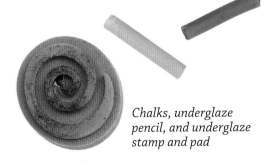

Chalks, underglaze pencil, and underglaze stamp and pad

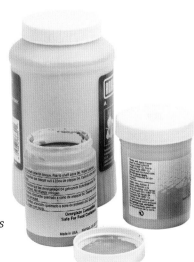

Overglazes

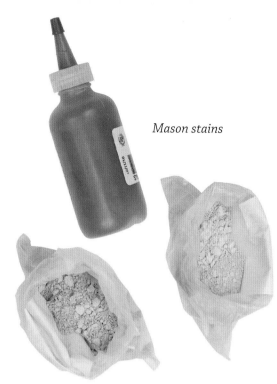

Mason stains

Raku

Raku glazes are specially formulated for the shock of the fast-cooling raku process, in which the beads are taken out of the hot kiln and placed into a reduction chamber with a combustible material. The fast cooling makes the glaze crack, and the carbon in the smoke fills the fine cracks for a crackled effect. Raku is a lot of fun and always a bit unpredictable in its results (see below right photo).

Mason Stains

Mason stains are colorants that you can add to clay, glaze, or slip (a mixture of clay and water) for decorating. In some of the projects later in the book, you'll be adding them to slip for color (see top right photo).

Luster

Luster is a glaze that you paint over an already overglazed and fired bead. You then fire it to a really low temperature, usually cone 022. Lusters give a metallic finish to the beads (see bottom right photo).

Because they are fairly expensive, they are usually used sparingly.

Majolica Glazes

Majolica glazes give another unique effect. You paint an opaque white glaze on the bead. Once it's dry, you paint underglazes on top of the white glaze. When the pieces are fired, the colors soak into the white glaze (see above right photo).

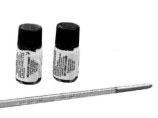

Luster glaze materials

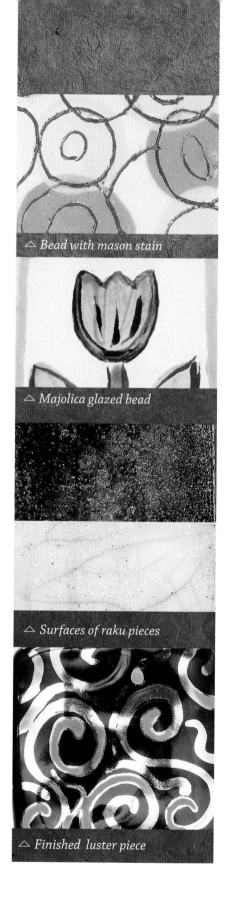

△ *Bead with mason stain*

△ *Majolica glazed bead*

△ *Surfaces of raku pieces*

△ *Finished luster piece*

Decals

Decals are printed stickers that you apply to a glazed and fired bead (see top right photo). Then you re-fire the bead at approximately cone 016 for permanency. You can find decals at ceramic supply stores or online. You can also make your own custom decals or have them made for you.

Greenware Tools

The tools and materials in the following sections are all those you'll use to work with clay when it's still "green"—that is, not yet fired. As you begin making beads, you'll get a feel for what tools you'll need. It all depends on what techniques you find yourself repeating and which tools can help you work faster and smarter.

Fabric Work Surfaces

Clay sticks to plastic and other smooth surfaces, so you'll need to put a piece of fabric under the clay while you work. Canvas is often used in traditional ceramics, but it can leave marks in the clay. If you want a smoother surface, use approximately one yard of smooth cotton. Fold the cotton in half once or twice so it's several layers thick. After you've been working on it for a while, the fabric is likely to become damp. Refold it to get a dryer surface and to prevent the clay from sticking.

Plaster Boards

You'll need a surface to set your beads to dry. If you are making flat beads, it's better to dry them between two boards, which will prevent the clay from drying too fast and warping. Plaster board is great for drawing the moisture out of the clay consistently. I make my boards by cutting a large piece of drywall board into manageable rectangles. Then I run a strong tape around the edges to prevent the plaster from leaking out of the boards. If plaster gets into your clay, it will explode in the kiln.

For drying clay, you can also use two wooden boards with newspaper layered in between. It's not as good as plaster board, but the wood-and-newspaper trick is a quick and easy way to get started.

△ *Detail of finished piece with decal*

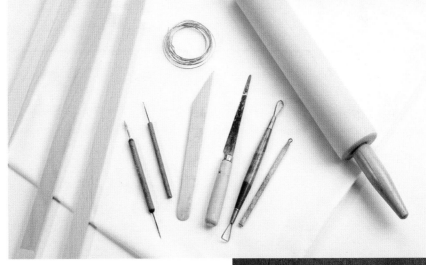

△ *Ceramic tools and a fabric work surface*

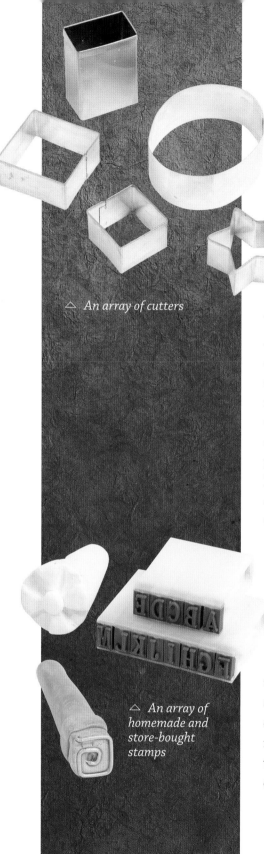

△ An array of cutters

△ An array of homemade and store-bought stamps

Plastic

Use plastic sheeting or a heavy-duty garbage bag that you've cut along the sides to cover your beads when they are drying. If the bead shapes are three-dimensional and you can't easily dry them between plaster boards, the plastic helps them dry slower and more consistently.

Wire Tools

A wire tool has two small wooden dowels for handles surrounding a long wire attached in the middle. You use a wire tool for cutting clay off the block. You can make one yourself by tying piano wire to two wooden sticks. Drill a hole through the middle of each stick and secure the wire to the stick through the hole.

Needle Tools

You use a needle tool for cutting out bead and pendant shapes. This is the tool I use the most. Like an awl, a needle tool has a handle with a needle coming from the center. Needle tools come in several sizes. The finest one doesn't disturb the clay as much as a larger needle does, which is perfect when working with small beads. You can make one of these yourself by drilling one end of a 6-inch-long (15.2 cm) dowel rod and inserting a needle. Secure it with a little glue.

Cutters

Cookie cutters make it easy to quickly cut out pendants. I suggest buying polymer clay cutters at a craft store, or petit four cutters from a cooking store. You'll find that gourmet cooking stores offer many cutters and tools that you can convert into working with clay. The best cutters are those without tops, as they allow you to gently push the clay out of the cutter.

Stamps

You can push stamps of all kinds into the clay to make decorative impressions. Later, I'll show how you can easily design and make your own stamps. Overglazes look great when they break over a stamped texture, and it's fun to collect as many designs as you can.

Skewers and Straws

You'll need skewers and straws to make the holes in your ceramic beads. Collect a variety of sizes to keep on hand. I buy them at grocery stores, and I always keep my eyes open for new sizes when I eat at restaurants.

Rolling Pins

While you're at the cooking store, pick up a rolling pin to roll your clay flat. Make sure you get a wooden one so the clay won't stick to it, as it will with plastic or rubber. Larger, heavier rolling pins make it easier to roll clay. Of course, if you're lucky enough to have access to a slab roller, use it!

Wood Slats

Wood slats are simply two pieces of wood you use as guides. You push the rolling pin over the slats, with the clay on the surface between them, to create a flat piece of clay with a consistent thickness. I use two pieces of pine I bought in the craft wood section at my local hardware store. I start by rolling my piece of clay to about ¼ inch (6 mm) between the slats. Then I can remove the slats and roll the clay thinner if necessary.

Rulers

Any type of ruler or polymer clay measuring tool works for making beads a consistent size.

Slip Trailers

A slip trailer is a squeeze bottle with a fine hole at the top. You fill the bottle with slip and squeeze it out onto the clay for decoration.

Extruders

Extruders are basically bigger versions of those toys you may have used for playing with clay when you were younger. They come in a variety of sizes, from very small ones that produce a spaghetti-like string of clay, to large wall-mounted ones that extrude large coils up to 3 inches (7.6 cm) in diameter. I prefer a mid-sized extruder with a number of different-sized caps or plates. This kind of extruder looks and works just like a caulking gun. You insert the clay and screw on a plate with the hole size you want, then you pump out the clay just as you would with a caulking gun.

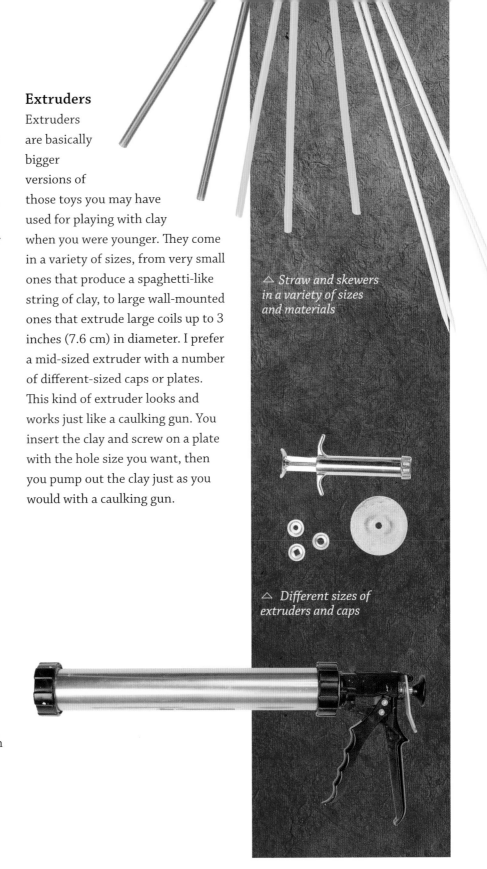

△ *Straw and skewers in a variety of sizes and materials*

△ *Different sizes of extruders and caps*

Basic Glazing Tools

To apply glazes, you'll need some tools to put on the glaze, and others to hold the beads in place as you do. When it comes to a work surface for glazing, I find that newspaper works just fine. After I'm finished with one project, I can simply throw the newspaper away, and I have a clean surface to work on again.

Brushes

Glazing jobs will require a variety of paintbrushes. Use a detail brush for working on small surfaces, and a larger brush for applying overglazes. Make sure your larger brush has soft bristles, so you don't accidentally scratch the decoration of an underglaze. Using high-quality brushes makes for an easier job and better results.

Skewers

In addition to the skewers you need for making holes, you'll need several for holding the beads while you're glazing. I buy packs of 100 at the grocery store and reuse them over and over. The skewer has to be thicker than the hole of the bead to keep the bead from sliding down. The longer, 10-inch (25.4 cm) skewers work well for glazing, as they are easy to manipulate.

Stands

You'll need something to stand the skewers against when you are glazing. You can drill holes into a board that are a little larger than the skewers, or you can pierce a wet piece of clay with similar holes. One method that works great: fill a flowerpot with sand to hold the skewers upright. Any of these ways will work, as long as the beads on the skewers don't touch each other.

Water Containers

Keep water in a nearby container to rinse out your brushes in between glazes. I save my sour cream containers for this. You can throw them out after a lot of glaze builds up on the bottom.

Sponges

You'll need a few sponges to wipe the dust off your bisque and to wipe excess glaze off your beads. Buy the cellulose sponges that don't have a scratchy side so you can use both sides of the sponge. You can pick these up at any grocery store, and be sure to keep several on hand at all times.

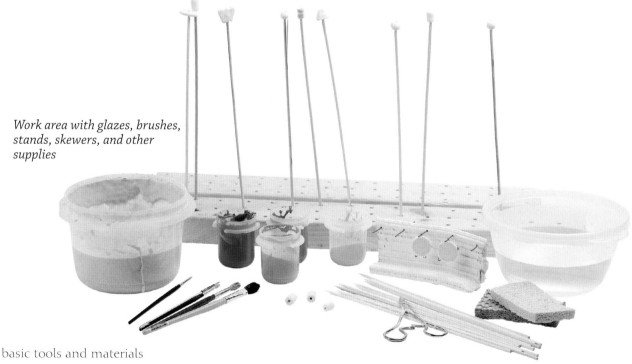

Work area with glazes, brushes, stands, skewers, and other supplies

Reamers

A reamer, or hole cleaner, has a wooden handle with a drill bit tool attached. You push a reamer in and out of the bead hole to clean out any clay or glaze that has found its way in there. I find these tools are also great for cleaning out any rough spots in a bead at any stage in the process.

Hemostats

Hemostats, used in the medical profession, make great tools for holding beads without holes. They have tweezer-like ends that lock to hold a bead securely while you're glazing. You can find them at medical or scientific supply stores.

Kilns and Kiln Equipment

For anyone just getting started in ceramics, a kiln is your biggest investment. The good news is that kilns last a really long time. Small kilns are becoming more readily available because of the popularity of lampworking, fusing, and metal clay. If buying a kiln isn't an option, many art centers or paint-your-own-pottery studios will fire your pieces for a small fee.

Electric kilns vary in size. Small test kilns, also called tabletop kilns, and annealing kilns are all electric. The beads in this book are all fired to cone 06, so before making the investment on your kiln, make sure it will reach this temperature.

The inside of the kiln also varies in size. Remember you'll need kiln furniture to support the beads when you are glaze firing, so take that into consideration when choosing your kiln. Test kilns are great because you can fire approximately twenty beads in the kiln and see the results quickly. A larger kiln requires more beads to fill it before firing. Another advantage of a test kiln is that it will most likely plug into a regular 110-volt socket.

Stilts

Stilts come in a variety of heights and widths. I use several 1 x 10-inch (2.5 x 25.4 cm) stilts, on which I rest the nichrome wire (see below) holding the beads. This way, I can stack several layers. You will also need stilts to hold up kiln shelves, if your kiln is large enough to have more than one shelf. I prefer 4-inch (10.2 cm) stilts for holding up my kiln shelves.

Nichrome Wire

Nichrome is a high-temperature wire made up of 80 percent nickel and 20 percent chrome. You can buy it at ceramic supply stores or from industrial wire supply

△ *Hemostat*

△ *Reamers*

△ *Electric kiln*

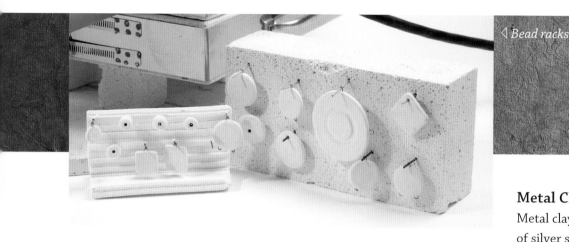

◁ Bead racks

locations. A 16-gauge wire works well for this job, though it's always nice to have several sizes on hand when loading your kiln.

Besides using it to hold pieces in a kiln, I use 24-gauge nichrome wire to make the loops that I insert into a wet clay bead to help link jewelry components together. In Chapter 2, I'll show you how to make these loops.

Bead Racks

Ceramic supply stores sell a variety of bead racks for the kiln, and you should be able to find something that works well in yours. I've also made several bead racks myself with clay and nichrome wire. One advantage of the homemade variety is that I can customize them to fit in all the odd spaces in my kiln (see photo above).

Above and Beyond

The previous sections cover all the basics you'll need for your Ceramic Tool Kit. From here to the end of the chapter, we'll go through some materials, tools, and supplies you may need depending on the techniques you're using and the projects you're making.

Metal Clay

Metal clay is made of small particles of silver suspended in organic matter and water. You form it with your hands, just as you would with clay. You can add metal clay to already-fired ceramics and then fire them again at a lower temperature. When you fire metal clay in a kiln, the organic matter and water burn away, leaving just the silver.

Metal clay in a finished piece and as a raw material

Tools for working with metal clay

Raku tools and equipment

Findings and other jewelry supplies

Raku Tools and Safety Equipment

"Low-fire" clay is a relative term—temperatures of around 2000°F (1093°C) are still awfully hot and potentially dangerous. Whenever you're around a hot open kiln, always protect yourself with a good pair of fireproof work gloves and safety glasses.

Be sure to use the right tools around the kiln as well. Raku tongs are helpful for grabbing hot bead racks out of the kiln. I actually use metal kitchen tongs for this purpose.

After a raku firing, you need to dump a hot rack into a bucket of combustible material. Sawdust, wood shavings, or leaves work well for this purpose. Make sure your bucket has a lid. I use metal feed bowls of various sizes that I bought from a hardware store. One lies over the top of the other to create the lid.

Basic Jewelry-Making Supplies

You'll be using a variety of jewelry-making supplies to make the projects in the book. Start collecting findings such as earring hooks, jump rings, crimps, closures, and beading wire. Ribbons and cords work well with ceramic beads, too.

To make and assemble the projects you'll need some basic jewelry tools, such as wire cutters, round-nose pliers, and crimps (see photos at right). In Chapter 5, we'll be using some of the above tools and materials when we go through a few basic jewelry construction techniques.

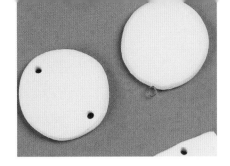

CHAPTER TWO

making the greenware bead

Now that you've gathered all the tools you need, let me show you some basic clay techniques. Hand-formed shapes create the foundation for a lot of beads, so I recommend you start by making these. Hand-formed beads are great in necklaces, but they're also great to test glazes on, something we'll discuss in Chapter 5. After you've mastered forming the basic shapes, we'll move on to joining clay, texturing the surface, and using high-temperature wire. Once you learn these basics, the sky's the limit in making ceramic beads.

Preparing the Clay

Now it's time for the fun part. Open up a bag of clay. Using a wire cutter, pull the wire taut and slice off a piece about the size of the palm of your hand (photo A). Remember that you're making beads, so you don't need too much. If you use less to start, the clay won't dry up too fast while you're working. Except for when you're actually cutting a piece from the block, keep the bag of clay tightly closed at all times.

Make sure the clay is the right consistency for making hand-formed beads. You want the clay to be wet enough so that it doesn't crack when you roll a ball and push it flat between your fingers (photo B). If it's too wet, the clay will stick to your fingers, leaving an unwanted texture on it. If the clay you have isn't the right consistency, cut another piece from a different part of the bag. I often find the clay in the middle of a 25-pound bag to have the best consistency for making hand-formed beads. Save the drier clay pieces for rolling out flat beads, something I'll show you later.

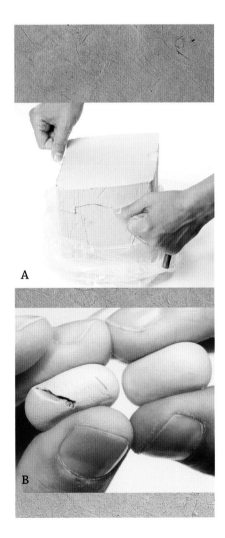

A

B

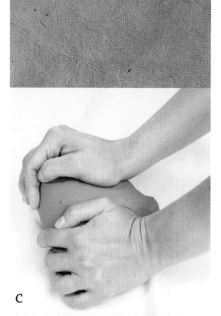

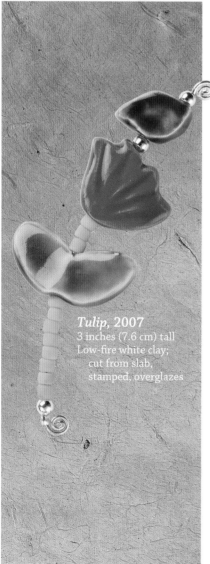

C

You can also change the consistency of the clay. If the clay is too wet, wedge it in your hands (photo C) or roll it around on a piece of canvas. Wedging clay is like kneading dough except that you should avoid introducing air into the clay body. Your hands and the surface fabric will draw the moisture out of the clay. If the clay is too dry—which is usually the case—place it in a plastic bag, poke some holes in the clay with a skewer, and then mist the clay with water. Close the bag tightly and recheck the consistency after a day, to see if it needs more water.

If you have clay that's bone-dry, without any moisture at all, you can place it in a bucket and cover it with water. After four to seven days, pour out any remaining water from the top of the clay, but do not pour any watery clay (called slip) down the sink drain—slip clogs drains! Pour the wet clay onto a piece of plastic or a plaster board and let it set up enough so that you can wedge it back to the right consistency.

Tulip, 2007
3 inches (7.6 cm) tall
Low-fire white clay;
cut from slab,
stamped, overglazes

Checking for Shrinkage

All clays shrink. It occurs when the water is leaving the clay body. This happens when the piece of work is drying and then even further when the piece is being fired in the kiln. Unfortunately, there is no way to know exactly how much your clay will shrink without doing a test. The good news is that the test is pretty easy.

1. Roll out a slab of clay approximately ¼ inch (6 mm) thick. Cut a rectangle from the slab about 2 inches by 6 inches (or about 5 x 15 cm).

2. With a metric ruler, draw a line measuring 100 millimeters in length. Draw another line at the top and bottom of this line, as this will make it easier to measure things later.

3. Let the slab dry flat and then fire it in the kiln. You should fire it to the highest temperature you will be firing your actual beads to. For example, the projects in this book are all low-fire, so the bisque firing is the hottest temperature the clay will reach. On the other hand, if you were using a high-fire porcelain then you would fire your test tile to the cone that the porcelain glaze would require.

4. After you have fired the test tile, use the same metric ruler to measure the line. If the line is 95 millimeters long, then your clay shrank 5 percent. A measurement of 91 millimeters means that the clay shrank 9 percent.

Now that you know how much your clay will shrink, and you've gotten it to the right consistency (as described in the previous section), you're ready to start making beads.

Holes vs. Wire

When you're making beads for jewelry, you have to decide how you want to string them together. Putting a hole in the bead is the most obvious and often the best solution. If you are making a flat bead or a charm, however, a wire loop may be a better choice. This is one great advantage of ceramic bead making: the high-temperature wire provides nearly unlimited design options. Once you've fired the bead in the kiln, you embed the wire permanently into the clay. In the following sections, we'll cover what you need to know when making holes or adding wires.

Making a Hole

Bead holes take some thought. Consider the diameter of your stringing material: will it be a fat cord or a skinny wire? You'll also need to take shrinkage into account—most beads will shrink between 5 and 6 percent. Because you have to fire beads on a high-temperature nichrome wire, the hole ought to be at least double the diameter of that wire. On the other hand, if you make the hole too large, the inside of the bead will show in the finished project.

After thinking about all of the above, determine which size skewer or straw is best for making the size hole you want. Insert the skewer halfway through the bead. I like to twist the skewer a little; it helps preserve the bead's shape. Gently pull out the skewer and insert it into the other side of the bead, twisting it all the way through. If you're having problems making the two holes line up, push a pointed skewer through the bead first. Twist it through until the point starts to come out the other side. Then finish the hole on the remaining side at that point.

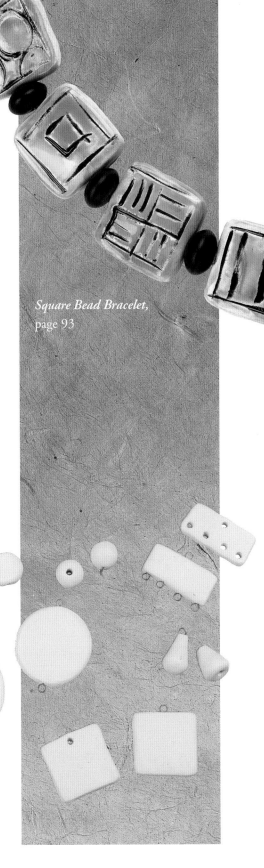

Square Bead Bracelet, page 93

Making Hand-Formed Bead Shapes

Hand-rolled bits of clay, simple and unadorned, make great beads by themselves. They can also be the foundation of very detailed and ornate beads. Start by rolling a piece of clay between the palms of your hands to form a ball. Most bead shapes you'll make begin with a simple ball, so practice making a good ball, and the other shapes will come easier.

To make a cylinder, place your finger on the top center of a ball. Roll it back and forth on a fabric surface while applying slight pressure. You'll form a cylinder with smooth, slightly rounded ends. If necessary, flatten each end. To make a cone bead, put your finger slightly off the bead's center and roll it as you did the cylinder (photo D).

Now it's time to get creative. Squares, triangles, circles, and diamonds all begin with a simple ball shape. With your thumb and forefinger, press a clay ball into

a flat circle. If cracks appear, the clay is too dry. You can most likely smooth out small cracks with the tip of your finger; just wet your finger and smooth the clay. Be careful not to use too much water, or the clay will become too wet. If that happens, you'll spend even more time trying to smooth the bead's surface. For really deep cracks, start over with a wetter piece of clay. I speak from experience—this advice will save you a lot of headaches.

To make triangles, use the forefinger and thumb of one hand and the forefinger of the other to press a flattened ball into a triangle (photo E). You make squares basically the same way. To make the faces of the beads flatter, press them on the work surface. And if you're trying to make beads uniform in shape and size, roll out a coil. Using a ruler as a guide, first mark and then cut the coil with your needle tool (photo F).

Adding High-Temperature Wire

To make high-temperature wire inserts, bend a loop near the end of a length of nichrome wire, cut it off the spool, and insert it into the clay. I find that 24-gauge wire works best. Try not to wiggle the wire around too much; if you do, press the clay around it to tighten the wire. You can place a loop anywhere on a bead—wherever you want to attach it to a cord or hang other beads from it.

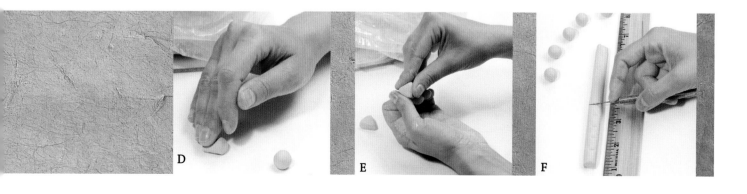

D

E

F

Using Ceramic Tools

When you're ready to go beyond hand-formed beads, you can use tools to create even more exciting shapes. For example, you'll find it's easier to build some beads in sections and put the pieces together later. Small wooden pottery tools come in handy for joining two pieces of clay.

To attach two pieces of clay, use the needle tool to scratch the surfaces of both pieces of clay where you intend for them to meet (photo G). Brush on a little water or slip with a plain old paintbrush. (See the sidebar at right to learn how to make slip to use as "glue.") Push the two pieces of clay together and give them a little twist or a bit of a wiggle. Finally, smooth the seam with the end of a small wooden clay tool (photo H).

Bead Crochet Bracelet, 2006
7 inches
(17.8 cm) long
Low-fire white clay;
hand-formed beads,
underglaze and
overglazes

H

Clay "Glue"

If you're joining a lot of pieces or having problems with seams cracking, use slip instead of water to join the clay. To make slip, take some scraps of dry clay and chop them up into small bits. Put this clay in a small airtight container and cover it with water. In a few days, the clay should have broken down into a thickened liquid called slurry. Carefully pour the water off the top of the slurry. Add a deflocculant (thinning agent) such as sodium silicate to the slurry, drop by drop. Stir the slurry between each drop until you get the consistency of white craft glue or heavy molasses.

G

Making Hollow Beads

Large beads made from ceramic material are sometimes too heavy to be practical. One solution is to make hollow beads. First, roll out a ball to the desired size. Cut the bead in half with a needle tool. Holding a half-sphere in the palm of your hand, carve out the inside with a ceramic tool that has a hook or a loop at one end (photo I), until the walls are ⅛ inch (3 mm) thick. Do the same to the other half-sphere.

Now score the two edges of the bead, add a little slip or water, and join them together. Smooth the joint together until it's invisible. Gently roll the bead on the work surface to get an even roundness back into the ball. The air inside the bead should keep it from collapsing when you roll it. Insert your skewer to make the hole through the bead. Once you've made the hole, set the bead aside to dry.

An important note: If you use nichrome wire instead of a hole in the hollow bead, you still need to pierce a small hole with your needle tool to let the air escape so the ball doesn't explode during the firing process.

Making Flat Beads

To make flat pieces of clay with a consistent thickness, you need to roll a slab. Position two wooden slats, no farther apart than the length of a rolling pin, on a fabric-covered work surface. Cut a thin, flat piece of clay off the clay block with a wire tool. Roll the rolling pin back and forth a few times over the clay, then turn the slab over and rotate it by a one-quarter turn. Repeat the rolling, flipping, and turning process until the slab is as thick as desired. If you follow these steps, the clay won't warp as much in the drying and firing process as it might otherwise.

Now you're ready to cut beads out of the slab. Use either a needle tool, dragging it through the clay to outline any shape, or a cutter, pressing it into the clay evenly. (An open-style cookie cutter works best.) Gently lift the clay shape out with your finger, trying not to mar or damage the surface. Smooth the rough edges with your finger (photo J).

Wire Work Pin, 2003
4 x 2½ inches (10.2 x 6.4 cm)
Low-fire white clay; cut from slab,
underglazes

Homemade Clay Cutters

You can buy cookie cutters almost anywhere, but you can make cutters easily yourself with aluminum or copper stripping. Draw a design on a piece of paper. Using round and square dowels or rods, bend the strip of metal to match your drawing, as shown in the photo. Trim the metal off with scissors so that the ends will overlap by ¼ inch (6 mm). Wrap a piece of clear tape around the cutter a few times where the two ends meet. You're ready to cut!

Making Extruded Beads

Extruders come with a variety of plates that determine the extruded shape. Experiment to discover what the extrusions produce. The larger wall-mounted extruders can even make hollow tubes. Once you choose a plate, take a piece of clay and roll into a cylinder that fits into the extruder. Fasten on the plate, insert the clay, and pump

K

L

the extruder until the clay comes out (photo K). With a needle tool, cut the extrusion into the desired lengths for the bead you're making. Smooth out the edges with your fingers and pierce the hole.

Making Beads with Press Molds

Press-molding is a good way to quickly make consistent beads. Measure out similarly sized pieces of clay for the mold. Roll each piece of clay into a ball and press it into the mold (photo L). If necessary, trim any excess clay off of the edges with a needle tool.

Raku Bracelet, **2007**
7 inches (17.8 cm) long
Low-fire white clay; cut
from slab, raku

Sticks, 2006
16 inches (40.6 cm) long
Low-fire white clay; hand formed,
underglazes

M

Removing Clay from Press Molds

If the press mold is made of plaster, the clay bead should come right out. If the mold doesn't release the clay right away, let it sit for a minute. The plaster draws moisture out of the clay, making the bead pop out easily after a while.

Plastic and rubber molds don't work as well for clay because the clay will tend to stick to their surfaces. If you want to use them, you'll have to experiment, as results can vary from mold to mold according to the detail of the beads. Another way to avoid stuck clay is to try putting a little cornstarch or a mist of olive-oil spray in the mold.

Making Your Own Press Molds

To make a plaster press mold, you need:

• Plaster

• The object you want to copy (such as a button)

• Oil soap

• A small cardboard box

• A disposable bowl for mixing the plaster

• A stirring stick

Before starting make sure you're nowhere near your bead-making area. As mentioned earlier, if plaster gets in your clay, it will explode in the kiln.

Find a cardboard box slightly bigger than what your mold will be. Flatten a piece of clay into the bottom of it. Press the object (such as the button) face up into the clay until the edges are flush. Brush the clay and object with the soap, which helps the plaster release the object. Fill the mixing bowl with enough warm water to fill the box. Pour the plaster in the bowl until it forms a peak that extends out of the water. Let the plaster sit for a couple of minutes and then mix well, taking care to not introduce air bubbles into the plaster (photo M).

Once the plaster has a good consistency, pour it into the box (photo N). Tap the side of the box with the stick to force the air bubbles to rise to the surface. Once no more bubbles rise, let the plaster dry. After the plaster has set, tear the box away and remove the clay and the object. You may need to clean the edges of the plaster with your finger or a knife to remove sharp edges. Set the mold aside to dry. Once it's completely dry, it's ready to use.

N

O

Drying and Clean-Up

You can set aside small hand-formed beads on a piece of plaster board to dry out in the open. A warm, sunny spot or a fan helps dry the beads if you're in a hurry, but don't try this with flat beads or beads with joints—they will crack for sure!

To dry a flat bead that does not have three-dimensional decorations on it, put it between two plaster boards to help keep it from warping (photo O). If the bead has a decoration on it, wrap it in plastic to help slow the drying process. Beads placed between two boards usually take a few days to dry, but it is worth the wait to prevent them from warping while drying or else later in the kiln. Humidity in the room also factors into the drying time. If in doubt, a good rule of thumb is, the slower the drying time, the better.

Once the beads are dry, you may still need to do some additional clean-up. Sand sharp edges with fine sandpaper or a fingernail file. Bead reamers are great for cleaning up the bead holes one last time before the initial firing. Since clay dust is not something you want to breath, keep the sandpaper, file, or reamer wet as you work. Better still, wear a mask.

Metal and Clay Pendant,
page 108

CHAPTER THREE

decorating beads

Producing different shapes is only the start of the magic of bead making. Decorating the bead is what completes the piece. Some decorating techniques need to be done when the bead is still in its greenware state, before you fire it. Others can be done only after you put the bead through its initial bisque firing.

Decorating the Green Bead

You use the following techniques while the bead is still wet or in the process of drying. Once you have decorated the bead, let it dry, and bisque-fire in the kiln. If you want, you can apply a clear glaze to seal and protect the beads at this stage.

Stamping

Stamps and texture sheets let you add great design elements while your beads are still damp clay. Texture sheets work especially well with overglazes because the glaze tends to pool in the design's grooves, creating depth and variety.

When it comes to creating texture in a bead, you have many options. You can press stamps into the wet clay after you've created the basic bead shape. You can roll balls, cylinders, and cones across a texture sheet. To get an even impression on each side of a flat bead, sandwich the bead between two stamps and apply pressure (photo A). You can press bisque, wood, or plaster into clay without any problems. Items from nature make great stamps too—

A

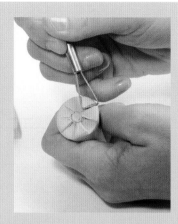
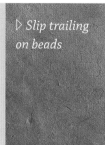
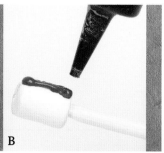

▷ *Slip trailing on beads*

B

C

Putting a Personal Stamp on Your Beads

Store-bought stamps can be great, but nothing beats the personal touch of creating your own unique stamps to decorate beads with. Here's how:

Roll a ball of clay into a big cone bead shape. Flatten the large end to be the face of the stamp. Now you can add clay to the face or carve into the clay to create your design. If you want to carve the stamp, wait until the clay has dried to a leather-hard state. After you've finished your design, bisque-fire the stamp in the kiln. After it's fired, it's ready to be used as a stamp.

you can press leaves or shells, for example, directly into the clay with great results. If you use a rubber stamp, add a little cornstarch or mist of olive oil to help release the stamp from the clay.

Slip Trailing and Slip Decorating

The opposite of stamping is slip trailing. Slip trailing creates a raised design on your bead that also works well with overglazes. Fill a slip trailer with slip (see page 25) and squeeze the bottle to apply a decorative pattern on the bead (photo B).

Slip decorating involves adding mason stains to slip you've made from the same clay body as the bead. Paint the stained slip onto a wet bead and let it dry. When the bead

is leather-hard, you can scratch or carve into the surface with a needle tool, revealing the clay beneath the surface, as shown in photo C. Let the pieces dry completely and then bisque-fire them.

Leaves and shells to use for stamping beads

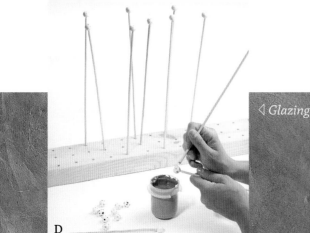

D

Decorating the Bisque-Fired Bead

Glazing is my favorite part of ceramic bead making. The options are limitless. Manufacturers are constantly formulating new colors and improving on the formulas to ensure consistent color after firings. Just browse your local ceramics store to get an idea of the many possibilities available. Most stores have glazed test tiles so you can see firsthand what the glaze looks like after being fired.

Before you begin glazing, make sure you have a clean work surface and clean water for your brushes. Take a damp sponge and wipe off your bisque-fired beads to remove any dust that might disrupt the glazed surface. Gently twist each bead onto a skewer securely and stand it up in your bead stand (photo D).

If your bead has a wire loop instead of a hole, you can glaze it by holding the wire loop in a pair of hemostats. When you are between coats, hang

Circle Choker, 2007
16 inches (40.6 cm) long
Low-fire white clay; cut
from slab, underglaze
and overglaze

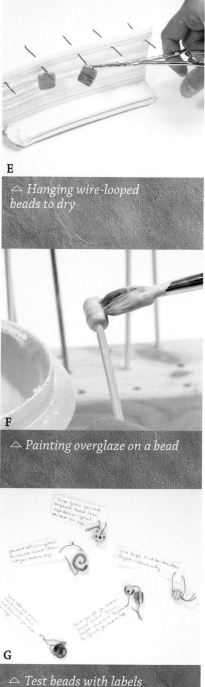

E

△ *Hanging wire-looped beads to dry*

F

△ *Painting overglaze on a bead*

G

△ *Test beads with labels*

the beads on a wire stand. I use a bead stand from the kiln for this (photo E). You are now ready to begin glazing.

Using Overglazes

You can apply overglazes by either dipping the bead or painting it. I prefer to paint overglazes; you have more control with the brush and can keep the glaze out of the holes. Painting also requires less clean-up.

Read the glaze instructions on the jar label. Usually, a glaze requires three coats for maximum coverage (photo F). Experiment with more and fewer coats, especially if you are glazing beads that have texture. Glazes sometimes break on a textured bead, creating great depth and variety. To help facilitate this process, use all those first practice beads you made. I like to

tie a note card on each practice bead describing how I applied the glaze (photo G). These notes can be invaluable for future glazing.

If you want to dip-glaze your wire-loop beads, you'll probably need to water down the glaze first so that it is not too thick. With the bead on its skewer, dip it into the jar and pull it out quickly. If you leave it in the jar too long, the pores of the bead will absorb too much of the glaze. Pull out the bead and tap it on the side of the jar to knock off any excess glaze. Stand the skewer up in its stand and let it dry.

For both methods of glazing, you need to clean up the bead once the glaze has dried enough to touch. Gently twist the bead off its skewer and clean around the hole with a pointed ceramic tool, a bead reamer, or a damp pipe cleaner.

Using Underglazes

Underglazes stay put better than overglazes. The color you see in the jar is more likely to be the color you get, which makes it easier to visualize what your finished bead will look like. You can paint underglazes on beads with one coat or as many coats as you want. I like to use tiny brushes to get fine detail. If you're intimidated by the thought of detail painting, especially when you're just starting out, use a regular pencil to draw guidelines right on the bead. The graphite will burn off during the firing.

To paint horizontal stripes around the bead, rest the bead's skewer on the side of the water bowl or glaze container. Load your brush with underglaze and hold it steady, just touching the bead, while you rotate the skewer with your other hand (photo H). Slowly pressing the brush onto the bead creates a steady, consistent stripe.

If you'd like to make polka dots, get out the skewers again. Dip the flat end of a skewer into the underglaze and press it onto the bead (photo I). This method produces nice round dots every time.

Using Stamps, Pencils, and Chalks

Underglaze stamp pads are made with a sticky underglaze-soaked sponge pad. Pencils and chalks (also called chalk crayons) are basically dried underglazes compacted into a stick form. All these forms of underglaze work better if you bisque-fire the bead immediately after you apply them, as that will stabilize the underglaze. Only after this step should you apply a clear overglaze to the bead. If you don't have the time to bisque-fire the beads again, sponge the clear glaze on instead of brushing it on. This technique helps to prevent the underglaze from smearing.

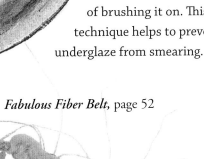

Fabulous Fiber Belt, page 52

△ *Painting horizontal stripes*

△ *Adding dots to a bead with the end of a skewer*

Clear-Glazing

Clear-glazing has two positive effects: it makes a bead stronger and also seals the pores to keep out dirt. Clear glazes come in shiny or matte finishes. Because they are a type of overglaze, you apply clear glazes the same way as the colored overglazes described on page 34. If you're concerned about fine detail or if you don't want to smudge any pencil or chalk work, you can bisque-fire the beads again to stabilize the colors before applying the clear glaze.

Most underglazes do not contain flux, so you can load them into the kiln just like greenware beads. Read the underglaze jar label. Some underglazes, after a few coats, develop a gloss finish after being fired. Load beads with these glazes into the kiln as if they were overglazed (see the section on page 42 in Chapter 4).

Using Majolica Glazes

Majolica glazes add detailed decorations to a bead's surface. Unlike the other surface-decorating techniques here, you add majolica glaze underneath the colorants (colored glazes). To do this, first paint an opaque white majolica glaze onto a bead's surface. After it has dried, paint on the colored majolica glazes over it (photo K). These glazes behave like underglazes and are used the same way.

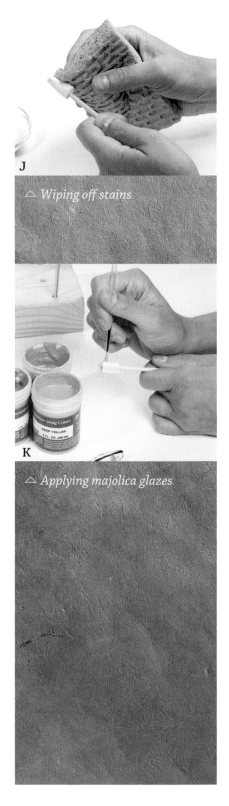

J

△ *Wiping off stains*

K

△ *Applying majolica glazes*

Flowery Fun, **2004**
Pendant: 6 inches (15.2 cm) long. Low-fire white clay; cut from slab, hollow beads, underglazes

Using Stains and Oxides

Stains and oxides are raw materials. You don't use them on their own when bead making, but you can mix them into glazes, slips, and the like. If you want to, you can water down stains and oxides, paint them on a bead, and then wipe them off the surface. This technique leaves the stain in the texture of the bead (photo J).

Adding Decals

Decals can be a lot of fun. You can find vintage ceramic decals online and at ceramics supply stores. You can also have custom decals made.

Before you add a decal to a bead, you have to apply a glaze to the bead and fire it. When the bead is ready, follow these steps:

1. Trim the decal as close to the design as possible to avoid excess on the bead. Soak it in water until the paper backing comes off.

2. Keeping the decal in the water, submerge the bead and carefully slide the decal onto it (photo L). As long as the decal and bead remain underwater, you can position the decal however you like.

3. When you're satisfied, remove the bead and decal from the water and carefully push any air or water out from underneath the decal.

4. Fire the bead again, this time to approximately cone 016—as always, though, be sure to follow the manufacturer's firing guidelines.

L

△ *Applying a decal*

Flower Power Necklace,
page 63

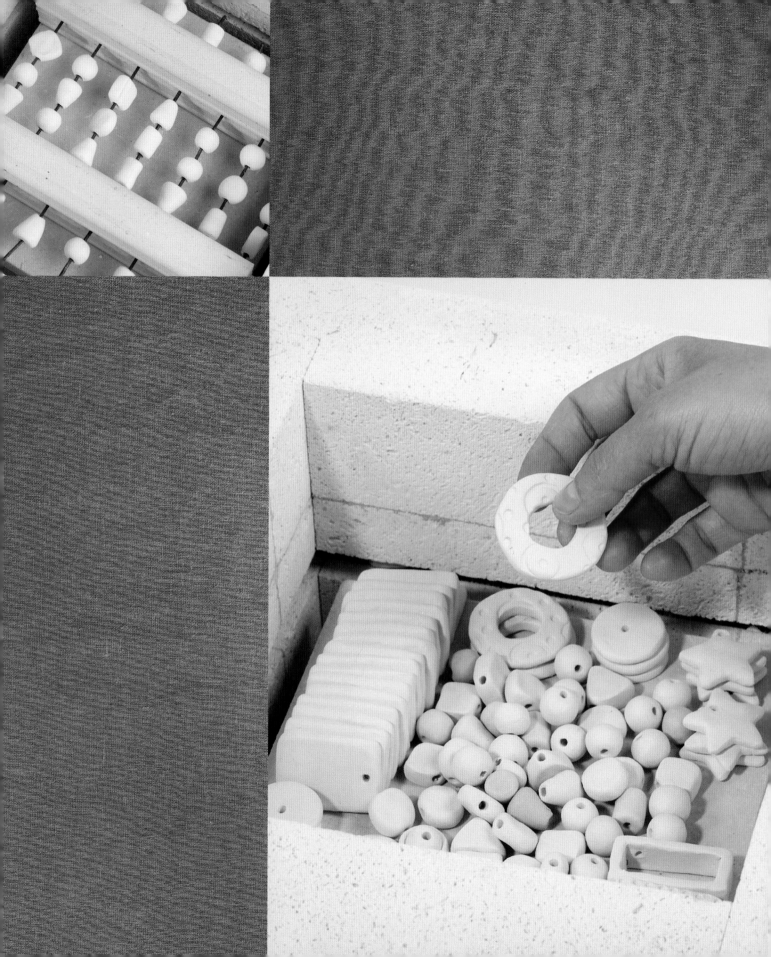

CHAPTER FOUR

bisque firing and glaze firing

We've talked at various places in the first three chapters about firing your beads. In this chapter, we'll get into the nitty-gritty of how (and why) to fire your beads.

Bisque firing is the first of two kiln firings in the bead-making process. It transforms greenware into a more solid state called bisque. Glaze firing, the second firing, turns painted clay beads into shiny, finished ceramic beads suitable for jewelry.

Bisque Firing

When you bisque-fire clay, it makes it stronger, which facilitates the glazing process. Bisque firing also releases most of the gases in damp clay. If the gases are still present in subsequent firings (such as glaze firings), they will try to escape through the glaze, which can cause tiny holes and craters on the surface of your bead.

The Transformation Process

The temperature range for firing a bisque kiln is usually in the low-fire range. When the temperature reaches about 1900°F (1038°C), a transformation in the clay takes place—the water and organic matter burn off and the clay molecules fuse together. This process makes the bead strong.

If you fire the beads to a higher temperature, the molecules fuse together so much that the beads cannot accept any glaze. So the low-fire range works best for bisque firing. Bisque-fired beads still have pores that can absorb the glaze, making a tight fit. In this book, we'll work with low-fire glazes, which are typically fired to cone 06, or 1828°F (998°C). I like to fire my bisque kiln

◁ *Loaded kiln shelf with bowls and pieces arranged evenly*

▷ *Loaded kiln shelf with flat beads stacked and arranged sideways*

A

B

to cone 04, or 1945° (1063°C). This setting makes the beads as strong as possible while still being able to accept glaze.

Loading a Kiln for Bisque

By definition, greenware beads are not glazed; therefore, you can load them into the kiln however you like, even one on top of the other. Just be sure the beads aren't touching any elements that can damage the kiln. Load the kiln evenly, so the air can circulate and the gases can escape. This way, the kiln can also heat up evenly, ensuring that all the pieces inside reach the proper temperature.

Here are a few tricks for organizing your beads in the kiln and making it easier to unload later:

• Place little beads, like balls and other shapes that might roll around, into a small unglazed pinch pot or a terracotta flower pot.

• Stack flat pieces on top of each other. If you have so many that the stack might fall over, turn

them on their sides, but keep them pushed up against each other to prevent warping.

• If you have a really large piece to fire, lay it flat on a kiln shelf. Don't stack too many pieces on top or the weight could damage the piece when it shrinks during the firing.

Another thing to watch for: If you put nichrome wire in any of your pieces, keep the wire away from other beads. If the wire touches another bead, it could cause a black

stain on the bisque. Photos A and B show two properly loaded shelves in a bisque kiln.

Typical Schedules for Bisque Firing

You should refer to your kiln manual for the recommended firing schedule. If you don't have a manual, contact the manufacturer and ask them to send you one. A typical schedule varies from kiln to kiln because of the size. If you want to get started without a manual, you

Cupid Ring, page 83

Flowers Galore, 2007
Pendant: 6 inches (15.2 cm) long. Low-fire white clay; formed and cut, underglazes

can use this book as a general guide, but remember that it won't be perfect for your individual kiln.

For firing a manual kiln, once you've loaded it, here are the basic steps:

1. Turn the dial to Low and leave the peephole unplugged. Leave it like this for at least two hours. If the pieces in the kiln are not completely dry, leave it on Low a while longer. To check if the water has left your beads, place a mirror over the peephole. If you still see condensation on the mirror, your beads aren't dry yet.

2. After you are sure the beads are dry, turn the dial to Medium for an hour and insert the peephole plug. After the hour, turn the dial to High for the remainder of the firing. When the kiln reaches the correct temperature, the sitter will drop, causing your kiln to shut off. If you're firing a digital kiln, a 400°F (204°C) per-hour climb is usually safe if the beads are dry.

3. Wait until the kiln has cooled completely before you unload it. If you open the kiln when it's too hot, thermal shock can cause little cracks in your glaze after the second firing-and by then it's too late. Better safe than sorry!

Glaze Firing

Usually, when you're making a ceramic bead, you do the following after the bisque firing. First, you paint an underglaze on a bead and let it dry. Then you cover the bead with a clear or colored overglaze, which is composed of crushed glass, called frit, suspended in solution. When the kiln reaches the frit's melting temperature, the liquid burns off and the glass melts, flowing together over the bead's surface to create a smooth and usually shiny surface. The following sections give you the steps and advice you need for this second firing.

△ *A kiln stilt with beads*

△ *Stacking posts and wires with beads*

△ *Glazed beads strung on wire and loaded onto posts*

Loading a Glaze Kiln

Loading a glaze kiln requires more planning than loading a kiln for bisque firing. Glazed beads should not touch each other or the sides of the kiln. Before learning how to load the kiln, though, let's find out what happens in the kiln during this firing.

As mentioned earlier, an overglaze melts over the surface of a bead. If the bead is glaze-fired beyond its temperature range, however, the glaze keeps flowing right off the bead and onto your kiln shelf. Because glaze is essentially molten glass, if two beads touch during the firing, they easily fuse together. How you load beads in a kiln for glaze firing, therefore, is very important.

A kiln stilt is a piece of bisque that has wire prongs to rest the glazed piece on it (photo C). If the beads have holes, you also use kiln posts in the bottom kiln shelf. Space the posts 2 to 3 inches (5.1 to 7.6 cm) apart. String several beads onto high-temperature wire and lay the wire down on the posts (photo D). High-temperature wire only sags a little during a cone 04 firing. To prevent your beads from sagging and hitting the shelf, place another set of stilts on top of the previous two (photo E).

To fire a really large bead, place it as close to the post as possible. Its glaze will bubble a little during the firing process, so ⅛ inch (3 mm) is close enough. Place post on top to hold down the wire. You can stack another layer of bead-loaded wires on top of the second stilts. Keep layering these until you reach the top of the kiln or you run out of beads.

Hanging Beads in a Kiln

Larger beads, and beads with wire loops, should be hung on a bead rack during firing. You can make bead racks several different ways. You can make a stand from clay and pierce it with nichrome wires, or you can make one from a piece of firebrick. Firebrick is a soft brick used to line ceramics kilns. You can purchase them from ceramics supply stores by the piece. Cut nichrome wires 2 inches (5.1 cm) long and push them into the soft brick.

Another way to hang beads with small holes is to make an S-shaped wire hook and hang the bead on the end of the hook. Rest a straight nichrome wire across two stilts and hang the other end of the hook on the wire.

Use stilts for a bead with a large hole that is completely glazed. Place the bead on the smallest stilt that will work. After the firing, the bead will have a few small pinholes, but you can sand it lightly to remove the sharp edges.

Firing a Glaze Kiln

Once you've loaded the kiln, you are ready to begin firing. Low-fire glazes are usually fired to cone 04–06, but read each glaze jar for specific temperatures. The firing process is shorter for glazes than for bisque because the beads no longer have any moisture to burn off. Consequently, you can turn up the kiln's temperature faster. Once again, refer to your kiln manual, but a typical climb in a digital test kiln is 400°F (204°C) per hour. If you are firing a manual test kiln, turn the kiln up a notch every half hour from Low to High.

Once the kiln has reached temperature, the cone will shut it off. Leave the kiln to cool completely to prevent thermal shock to the glazes. Once you can touch the beads with your hands, you can unload the kiln. This is the most exciting part of the whole process! It's so much fun to open the lid and see all of your creations transformed. The beads should slide easily off the wires and are ready for use. If a bead stubbornly sticks to a wire, grab the wire with a pair of pliers and gently twist the bead off with your hand. If necessary, you can clean off the sharp areas with a reamer. If the bead is really stuck, you might just have a new potted plant decoration instead of a usable bead!

Toggle Bracelet, 2005
7 inches (17.8 cm) long
Low-fire white clay; cut from slab, overglazes

CHAPTER FIVE

ceramic and jewelry-making techniques

The ceramic techniques in this chapter go beyond the usual ceramic bead making process. In the next few pages, I explain the processes that can take your beads to the next level. These processes include lusters, raku, and metal clay. These techniques will open a door to many new ideas for you. We'll finish up the chapter with a few techniques you'll need to know for putting together your remarkable beads into stunning jewelry.

Lusters

You paint lusters directly onto a bead after it has been glaze-fired. I use a fine brush to paint on the lusters to achieve greater detail. Because of the strong odors, you need to apply luster glazes in a well-ventilated area.

To begin, wipe the bead clean with alcohol (photo A). Brush on two coats of luster with a brush; the lusters are oil based, so they will take longer to dry. Let the beads dry overnight in a well ventilated area. Load them into the kiln on bead wires, as you did for the glaze firing.

During the firing, leave the kiln cracked open for ventilation—the lusters need oxygen to work. Place a stilt on its side to prop the lid open if your kiln doesn't have a support. Follow the temperature guidelines on the luster bottle to fire the kiln. The temperature is usually between cone 019 and 022. Once the kiln has reached temperature, you can close the lid of the kiln for the beads to cool slowly. Unload the kiln once it has reached room temperature.

△ *Preparing to apply luster*

Raku beads

Raku

Raku is an exciting process of Japanese origin. It involves moving the hot beads from your kiln into a metal container of sawdust or other combustible material. When the sawdust burns, it creates great variety within the glaze as the flames whip around the beads. Some glazes produce an effect not unlike an oil slick on the beads, as in the beads shown above.

To begin the process, place your kiln outside, along with a bucket of sawdust with a lid, a hose or bucket of water for any flare-ups, metal tongs for grabbing the beads, and kiln gloves. After glazing your beads with the raku glaze, load them into the kiln just as you would load them for a glaze firing. Keep in mind you'll need to grab the beads with

tongs when they are hot, so plan ahead, placing the wires so they will be easier to grab. See photo B for an example of a clay rack I made with a loop at the top for the tongs to grab. With this rack, I can easily pick up a whole rack of beads at once.

Once you've loaded the kiln, fire it to temperature. You must stay with the kiln during the firing. When it reaches temperature, open the kiln and grab the rack with the metal tongs. Now comes the fun part. Place the hot rack into the sawdust and add a little more sawdust on top. At this point, the beads should be smoking, if not on fire. Put the lid on top of the bucket and let the sawdust smolder. Make sure the lid is on tightly, so that the fire can consume the oxygen within the bucket.

After thirty minutes, the fire should have burned up most of the sawdust and the smoke should be almost gone. Open the lid and pull out the rack. Hose off the beads to freeze the glaze, cooling it enough so you can touch the beads. If any sawdust is still stuck to the sides of a bead, carefully remove it with a brass brush.

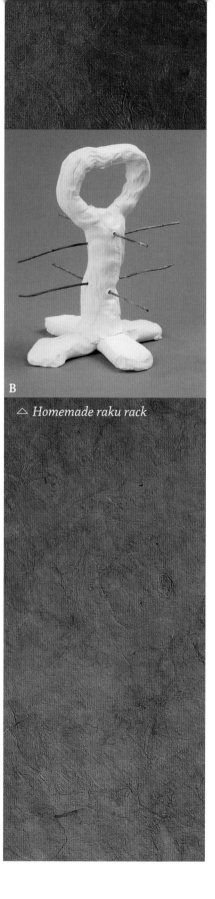

B

△ *Homemade raku rack*

Metal Clay

Metal clay comes in a variety of consistencies. You can paint a thin coat of metal clay paste onto bisque-fired ceramic beads or you can join metal clay slabs to a glazed bead. Experiment with different methods to see what results you can get.

To paint metal clay paste onto a bead, first wipe your bisque-fired bead with a sponge to remove any dust. Load your brush with the paste and paint a thin coat onto the bead. Let the coat dry. Repeat this process several more times, building up the metal clay on the bead. After you have a thick, consistent base, you can decorate the beads with metal clay applied through a syringe. Once the beads have dried, place them in a bowl of alumina hydrate and fire them to temperature.

You can add metal clay in its clay form to glaze-fired beads. Use plastic and glass ceramic tools for working with the clay, as metal ceramic tools will contaminate the metal clay. Roll out the metal clay on a glass cutting board. You can roll it out much thinner than you can ceramic clay, so use playing cards as guides to achieve a consistent thickness, just as you use wood slats for rolling out ceramic clay (see page 15). Metal clay has a stronger feel, even if thinner, than ceramic clay.

You can transfer most of the ceramic clay techniques you already know to metal clay. If the piece is flat, you can fire it directly on a kiln shelf. If the piece is round, you'll have to fire it in a bowl of alumina hydrate. Either way, fire metal clay pieces to the temperature recommended on the package.

After firing, the metal clay will have a white coating (photo C). Once the bead has cooled, brush or polish it to clean off the coating. If the pieces are compact, you can place them in a tumbler with stainless steel shot to clean them. The method I prefer is cleaning the metal clay with a brass brush, since I can do it quickly without the risk of chipping or breaking any small parts, as can happen in a tumbler. Silversmith suppliers sell a variety of attachments for your rotary tool that you can use for polishing metal clay to a shine.

Raku Pendant, 2007
Pendant: 1½ inches (3.8 cm) tall
Low-fire white clay; cut from slab, raku

C

△ *Metal clay bead in a bowl of alumina hydrate*

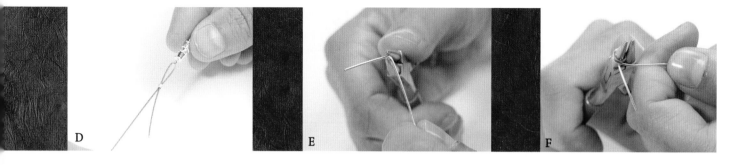

D E F

Jewelry-Making Techniques

Now that you have a stockpile of beads, it's time to start making jewelry. The projects in this book incorporate a wide variety of options for stringing and assembling jewelry. Each set of project instructions will list the supplies needed. The following sections explain some of the basic techniques you'll need to know.

Stringing on Beading Wire

Stringing bracelets and necklaces on beading wire is probably the easiest and most versatile way to create jewelry. To begin, layout your beads in the order you would like to string them. You can do this on a bead board (if you have one) so they don't roll around. When you get the desired length of beads for your piece, measure the beads, add approximately 4 inches (10.2 cm) to the number, and cut your beading wire to this length.

String a crimp bead onto the wire, followed by one end of the clasp. Bring the wire around and back through the crimp, as shown in photo D. Pull the wire firmly so the crimp is snug against the clasp. With flat-nose or crimping pliers, flatten the crimp so the wire can't move. String the beads onto the wire, making sure that the beads go over both wires. When you're ready to end the piece, string another crimp onto the wire, followed by the second piece of the clasp. Bring the wire back around through the crimp and through a few of the beads. Flatten the crimp, and trim the excess wire with wire cutters as close to the beads as possible.

Wire Work

If you are working with any kind of wire in your jewelry, you'll be creating the simple wire loop over and over again. To make a wire loop, get some round-nose and flat-nose pliers and wire cutters, and then follow these steps:

Tropical Colors Charm Bracelet, page 117

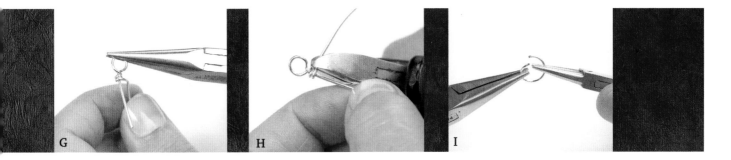

G   H   I

1. Make a 90-degree angle bend 1½ inches (3.8 cm) from the end (photo E).

2. With the pliers still in the bend, wrap the short end of the wire around the end of your round-nose pliers, making a complete circle (photo F).

3. Put the loop in your flat-nose pliers. Wrap the short wire around the long wire about three times (photo G).

4. If there is wire remaining you can snip it with wire cutters (photo H).

Jump rings are a type of jewelry finding that are often used with wire work. They are wire rings that can be opened for connecting two pieces. To open a jump ring, grab one side with flat-nose pliers and twist it open with either your fingers or another pair of pliers (photo I). Slide whatever you need to on the ring and twist the ring back together. It is important to twist the ring, because pulling the jump ring straight apart will misshape it.

Using Epoxy

Bisque is porous. For this reason, you'll want to use epoxy to adhere pin backs and earring posts to the back of a bead. If you are going to use epoxy on your bead, be sure that you do not glaze that portion of the bead.

Epoxy comes in two separate tubes. Squeeze equal amounts of each onto a paper plate. With a skewer thoroughly mix the two parts together, as in the photo below. Apply a little to the bead and the pin back. Push firmly together and let dry.

Mixing epoxy

boyfriend necklace

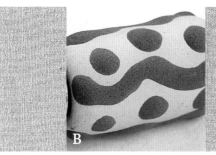

With a subtle color palette and unglazed finish, this necklace will look as good on your boyfriend as it does on you… well, almost.

tools and materials

Ceramic Tool Kit (see page 9)
Low-fire red or brown clay
Raised slip pen in black
4 decorative pewter spacer beads, 10 mm in diameter
18 inches (45.7 cm) of twisted rayon cord
Set of terminator crimps with hook clasps

step by step

1. Roll out a large ball of clay, approximately 1 inch (2.5 cm) in diameter. Roll this ball into an elongated bicone (see page 24 for information on rolling beads). Pierce a hole lengthwise in the bead (see photo A) and set it aside to dry.

2. Repeat step 1 to make two smaller balls of clay for the side bicone beads.

3. After the beads have completely dried, place the beads on skewers. With the slip pen, gently squeeze some squiggles and dots on the three beads (see photo B). Let the slip dry completely.

4. Take the beads off the skewers and slide them directly onto high-temperature wire. Suspend them in the kiln for firing. By placing them directly into the kiln, you minimize the chance of chipping off the slip while handling them. Bisque-fire the three beads.

5. Crimp one end of the hook clasp onto the rayon cord. String the three ceramic beads onto the cord with spacers in between (see photo C). Cut the cord to the desired length and crimp on the other half of the clasp.

fabulous fiber belt

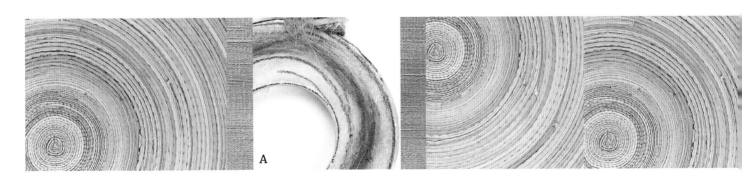

A

A stunning ceramic buckle links together a rainbow of vivid fibers to make this stylish belt.

tools and materials

Ceramic Tool Kit (see page 9)
¼ pound of low-fire white clay
24-gauge high-temperature wire, 1 inch (2.5 cm) in length
Underglaze chalks
Clear glaze
10 assorted fibers, 3 yards (2.7 m) in length
6 pewter circle beads, 10 mm

step by step

1. Roll a slab of clay to ⅛ inch (3 mm) thick and cut out the belt buckle with the donut cutter. Smooth the edges and insert a loop of high-temperature wire in one side, making sure the wire loop is large enough to thread all ten fibers through. Sandwich the buckle between two plaster boards and leave it to dry completely.

2. Hand-roll six ball-shaped beads, approximately ½ inch (1.3 cm) in diameter. Poke holes through the center of the beads, and set them aside to dry.

3. After bisque-firing the buckle and beads, apply the underglaze chalks in a circular pattern to the buckle and round beads. Apply two or three coats of the clear glaze. Dab the first coat on so the chalks don't smear (see photo A). Fire to the recommended temperature.

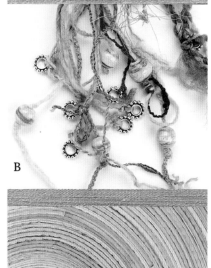

B

4. Suspend the round beads on a wire strung across two posts to fire them. Hang the buckle from a wire held by a fire brick. Glaze-fire to recommended temperature.

5. To assemble the belt, fold each of the fibers in half and push the loop through the wire on the buckle. Thread the ends of the fibers through the loop and pull the fibers snug.

6. To finish the belt, tie either a round bead or pewter circle bead to the ends of each of the separate fibers (see photo B).

cute as a button earrings

Because these earrings are simply press molded, it's easy to make a pair as a gift for every one of your friends.

tools and materials

Ceramic Tool Kit (see page 9)
Low-fire clay
High-temperature wire
Fine-grain sandpaper
Pink, lime green, and yellow underglazes
Button for making the charm mold
2 yellow, faceted Czech beads, 6 mm
2 sterling silver wire ear hooks
20-gauge sterling silver wire, 5 inches (12.7 cm) in length

step by step

1. Make a mold according to the instructions on page 28. I used a ½-inch (1.3 cm) button for the charm.

2. Roll a small ball of clay and press it into the mold. Remove any excess clay from the back before removing the charm from the mold. If the bead doesn't easily come out of the mold, stick the end of your needle tool into the clay and gently wiggle it out. Make two charms.

3. Make two small wire loops from the high-temperature wire (see page 24) and insert one into the top of each bead.

4. After the beads are dry, smooth any rough edges with a little sandpaper. Fire the charms in the kiln.

5. Paint a pink flower with a yellow center on the surface of the charm. Paint the outside and back of the charm with the lime green underglaze (see photo A). Apply two coats of clear glaze and fire again.

6. To assemble the earrings, make a wire loop on one end of the wire ear hooks. Slide a yellow bead onto the wire. Make another loop, but before closing it, slide on the charm. Repeat this step for the second earring.

twig brooch

Springtime colors and a long, graceful curve of wire create an eye-catching brooch. Wear it to plant an impression.

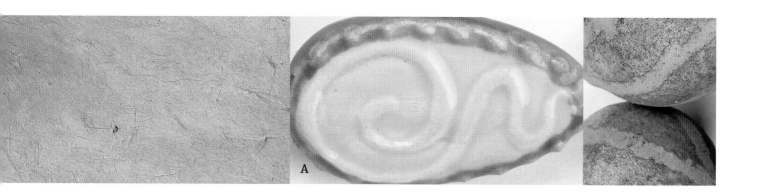

A

tools and materials

Ceramic Tool Kit (see page 9)
Low-fire white clay
Low-fire white clay slip
Yellow glaze
Terra-cotta glaze
Two-part epoxy
18-gauge sterling silver wire, 10 inches (25.4 cm) in length
5 glass olivine crescent beads, 6 mm in diameter
2 metal round beads, 5 mm in diameter
2 metal round beads, 3 mm in diameter
4 metal round beads, 2 mm in diameter
Pin back

step by step

1. Roll out a piece of clay to approximately ¼ inch (6 mm) thick. Cut out an oval about 1¾ inches (4.4 cm) long and 1 inch (2.5 cm) wide. Smooth the edges and send a skewer through the clay, from top to bottom.

2. Fill the slip trailer, then test the consistency of the slip on your work surface. Adjust the trailer until you get the slip to squeeze out easily, while it still retains its shape on the surface. Trail a squiggle and dot pattern over the surface of the bead (see photo A). Set it aside to dry. Be careful not to touch it until it's dry.

B   C

3. Bisque-fire the bead. Glaze the front of the bead yellow. Glaze the sides of the bead terra-cotta. Glaze just around the edge of the bottom. Leave the center of the back unglazed, which will help the epoxy to adhere to the bead later.

4. Glaze-fire the bead by suspending it on a wire supported by two stilts.

5. Before you assemble the pin, mix the two-part epoxy. When it's ready, apply it to the pin back and adhere it to the back of the bead. Set the pin aside until the epoxy has cured.

6. Using round-nose pliers, wrap the end of the wire from the tip to begin the spiral. Keep wrapping this bend into a coil with the flat-nose pliers, until it's approximately ¼ inch (6 mm) in diameter (see photo B).

7. String the beads as shown in photos B and C. Then make a large loop in the wire just above the last bead. After securing it (as shown on page 49), push the middle of the loop down to divide the loop into two ovals. Twist one of the ovals to secure them. With your fingers or the round-nose pliers, shape it into two leaflike loops.

blue dot bracelet

Simple wire wrapping transforms a basic donut bead of striking peacock blue into a stylish cuff.

tools and materials

Ceramic Tool Kit (see page 9)
Low-fire white clay
Peacock blue low-fire glaze
14-gauge sterling silver wire, 16 inches (40.6 cm) in length
20-gauge sterling silver wire, 40 inches (101.6 cm) in length

step by step

1. After rolling out a piece of clay ⅓ inch (8.5 mm) thick, cut out a circle about 1½ inches (3.8 cm). Cut a hole about ½ inch (1.3 cm) in the middle to create a donut shape. Smooth the edges of your donut and press a pattern into both sides of it with a texture stamp (see photo A). Bisque-fire the bead.

2. Paint the bead with three coats of the blue glaze. To fire this bead in the kiln, you will need to rest the bead on a stilt. Use the smallest stilt possible to minimize stilt marks after the firing. Fire the bead in the kiln to the recommended temperature on the glaze bottle.

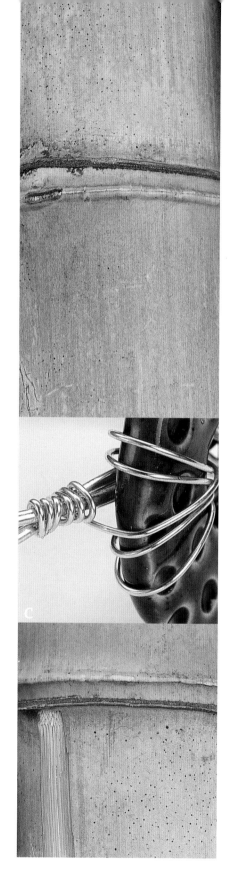

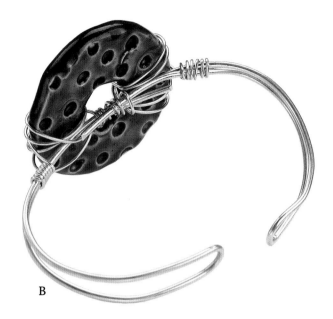

B

3. Take the piece of 14-gauge wire, and bend it at about 4 inches (10.2 cm) from each end toward its center (the cut ends will cross). Fold the rounded loop ends in again, as shown in photo B.

4. Now that you have the double wire, bend it into an oval that will fit your wrist.

5. Find the center of the 20-gauge wire and wrap it around the center top of the bracelet you just fashioned. Wrap it around several times so that the two cut ends of the 14-gauge wire are concealed in the 20-gauge wire wrapping.

6. Center the donut bead on the bracelet. With your wire in the center of the donut, wrap each side of the donut five times with the wire. When you wrap each side for the last time, take the wire through the center and out to the side of the bracelet. Wrap the bead wire six or seven times around the bracelet wires to secure it (see photo C). Trim any remaining wire.

flower power necklace

*With daisy decals applied to ceramic coin beads,
this choker summons the summer of love.*

tools and materials

Ceramic Tool Kit (see page 9)
Low-fire white clay
Cookie cutter, 1-inch (2.5 cm) circle
High-temperature wire
Yellow underglaze
Clear glaze
Six flower decals
12 orange faceted beads, 8 mm
6 olivene faceted, round beads, 6 mm
20 sterling silver ball beads, 4 mm
20-gauge sterling silver wire, 40 inches (101.6 cm) in length
Sterling silver toggle clasp

step by step

1. Roll out a flat piece of clay about ⅛ inch (3 mm) thick. With the cookie cutter, cut out six circles. Smooth the edges. With the high-temperature wire, make 12 small wire loops (see page 24). Add a wire loop to opposite sides of each circle.

2. Bisque-fire the beads and then paint them with the underglaze and a coat of clear overglaze. The decals I used have a yellow background, and I chose a yellow underglaze to paint the beads with so the decals would blend into the background. Depending on your decals, you might need a different color. Fire the beads suspended in the kiln.

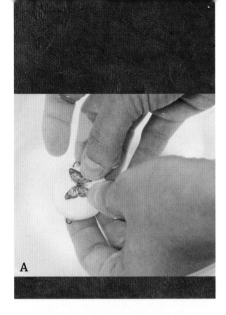

A

B

C

3. To add a decal to a bead, trim the decals to fit the beads and soak the decals in a bowl of water one at a time. After a minute or so, the decal will slide right off of its paper backing. Submerge a bead and slide the decal onto it. (Photo A shows this step using a different decal.) As long as the decal and bead are underwater, you can move the decal around. Once it's where you want it, take the bead out of the water. With your fingers or a sponge, gently press out any water or air that might have gotten trapped underneath, starting in the middle of the bead. Repeat this step for the rest of the beads.

4. Lay the beads on a kiln shelf (decal side up) and fire them to the recommended temperature, which is usually around cone 016.

5. To assemble the necklace, use simple wire loops to connect the beads together. Make a wire loop and connect it to one side of the toggle. Then string a silver, orange, olivine, another orange, and another silver bead (see photo B). Make another loop and trim the excess wire. Attach a third wire loop to the one you just made and string the same bead sequence again. This time, attach one side of a ceramic bead to the wire loop before closing it off.

6. Make a wire loop and attach it to the other side of the ceramic bead. String a silver, an orange, and a silver bead onto the wire. Attach the end to the next ceramic bead. Follow this sequence alternating the olivine and orange beads in between each ceramic bead (see photo C). When you have connected all of the ceramic beads, follow up with the two sequences of small beads, as described in step 5. Attach the second side of the toggle to the last wire loop.

multi-strand bracelet

Why settle for one strand? This bracelet joins five strands of colorful pebbles between two rectangular beads.

tools and materials

Ceramic Tool Kit (see page 9)
Low-fire red clay
High-temperature wire
Gold, lavender, and mint green colored slips
Fine sandpaper
Clear glaze
Beading wire
Amethyst chips
10 crimps, 1 mm in diameter
Golden jade pebbles
Olive jade pebbles
Red howlite pebbles
2 silver jump rings, 2 mm in diameter
Silver toggle

step by step

1. Roll out a flat piece of clay. Cut out two 1 x 2-inch (2.5 x 5.1 cm) rectangles. Add a loop of high-temperature wire to one of the long edges of the first rectangle. On the opposite edge, add five evenly spaced loops. Add the wires the same way to the second rectangle.

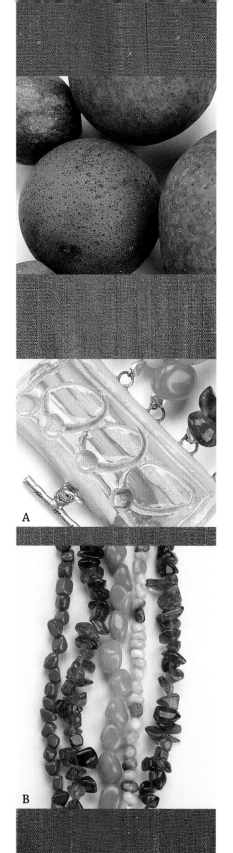

A

B

2. While the clay is still wet, paint on the slips. Coat one side of each rectangle with loose stripes, overlapping the colors. Let the rectangles dry to a leather-hard state.

3. With a carving tool, scrape the desired design into the rectangles. I outlined the rectangles and added some circles. With a skewer, I pressed small circles down one side (see photo A). Don't worry about rough edges when carving your design; once the beads have dried completely, you can lightly sand the edges smooth. Bisque-fire the rectangles.

4. After the first firing, add two coats of clear glaze and fire again.

5. Cut five pieces of beading wire, each 10 inches (25.4 cm) in length. Crimp one wire onto each of the five loops of one of the rectangles. String the top wire with the amethyst chips to the desired length, and then slide on a crimp. Send the wire through the loop of the second rectangle and back through the crimp. Test the length, remembering the toggle will add some length as well. When you have the correct size, crimp the bead.

6. Next, string the golden jade strand to the same length as the amethyst strand. Repeat the crimping process. String the third strand with olive jade, the fourth with amethyst, and the fifth with red howlite (see photo B).

7. Open up one of the jump rings. Slide it onto the outside wire loop of one of the rectangles and one side of the toggle. Connect the remaining toggle half onto the other rectangle with the second jump ring.

hot spot hair sticks

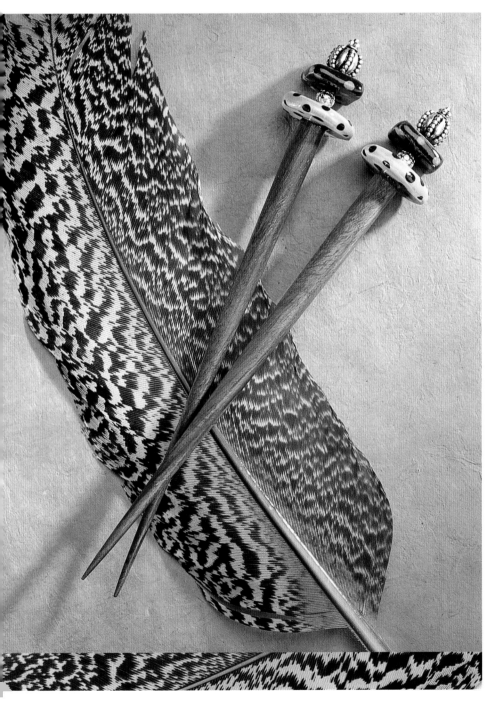

Tucked into an up-do, these polka-dotted hair sticks will start an instant party in your tresses.

A

tools and materials

Ceramic Tool Kit (see page 9)
¼ pound of low-fire white clay
Turquoise, dark brown, and light brown underglazes
Clear glaze
2 decorative sterling silver head pins, 3 inches (7.6 cm) long
2 pewter balls, 6 mm in diameter
2 sterling silver balls, 4 mm in diameter
2 wooden hair sticks, 6 inches (15.2 cm) long
Two-part epoxy

step by step

1. Hand-form two flat round and two flat square beads approximately 1 inch (2.5 cm) in diameter. Pierce holes through the face of all four beads. Set them aside to dry.

2. Bisque-fire the beads. Paint the two circle beads with the turquoise underglaze. Use the end of a skewer to add brown dots. Paint the square beads with the dark brown underglaze, and then add light brown dots.

3. Apply the clear glaze, and fire the beads to the recommended temperature.

4. To assemble the hair sticks, thread a pewter ball, the square ceramic bead, a sterling silver ball, and the round ceramic bead onto a head pin (see photo A). Trim the remaining head pin wire, leaving ¼ inch (6 mm) to insert into the hair stick.

5. Repeat the stringing sequence on the second head pin. Trim the head pin wire and set the stick aside.

6. Mix the two-part epoxy and apply it to the ends of the head pins. Insert each head pin into the end of a hair stick. To help hold the hair sticks upright while drying, place them in some clay or sand.

right on target earrings

When it comes
to fun accessories,
these winning
earrings score
a bull's-eye.

tools and materials

Ceramic Tool Kit (see page 9)
Low-fire white clay
High-temperature wire
Turquoise, lime, yellow, and black underglazes
Clear glaze
Pair of sterling silver ear wires

step by step

1. Divide a small amount of clay into five even amounts and roll them into five balls. Make sure they are all the same size, about ⅜ inch (9.5 mm) in diameter. Set two balls aside. Split one ball in half and roll each half into a new ball; set these two new balls aside. Remove and discard about a third of the clay from each of the last two balls, and re-roll the remaining clay into two balls. At this point, you should have six balls: two large, two medium, and two small.

2. Flatten the balls into disks. Smooth any cracks or rough spots.

3. With the high-temperature wire, make ten small wire loops (see page 24). Insert one in the top of a small disk for the ear wires. Insert another wire loop into the bottom of the same disk. Hemostats are helpful for holding onto the wire loops. Thread a new wire loop through this loop (at the bottom of the small disk) and insert it into the medium-sized disk. Do the same thing with another wire loop to connect the large circle to the medium circle (see photo A). Repeat these steps to create the other earring, and then carefully set both earrings aside to dry.

4. After bisque firing, paint the disks with the underglazes, starting with lime green for the bottom disk, then turquoise for the middle, and yellow for the top disk. Go back and make circular designs on the beads with the black underglaze (see the project photo).

5. Paint on the clear glaze, taking care to avoid getting any on the wire loops. If you need to clean glaze off the wire, use a wet paintbrush.

6. Hang the earrings in the kiln on wire and fire.

7. Add the ear wires to each earring.

A

majolica star earrings

Majolica glaze makes these earrings special. Wear them whenever you want to be the center of attention.

tools and materials

Ceramic Tool Kit (see page 9)
Low-fire red clay
Star cookie cutter
High-temperature wire
White majolica glaze
Royal, turquoise, and yellow majolica colors
2 blue seed beads
20-gauge sterling silver wire, 4 inches (10.2 cm) in length
1 pair of sterling silver ear wires

step by step

1. Roll out a piece of red clay about ⅛ inch (3 mm) thick. Cut out two stars with the cookie cutter. Smooth the edges and add a high-temperature wire loop at the top of each star. Bisque-fire the two stars.

2. Paint three coats of the white majolica glaze on the front and back of the stars. Hold the stars by the wire loops with hemostats, if you have them. With a sponge, wipe off the edges of the stars to show off the red clay.

3. Before glaze firing, paint the colors—one coat only—onto the stars with detail brushes. Outline the star in royal blue. Add yellow dots inside the blue star, and then paint a turquoise star within the dots (see photo A).

4. Fire the two stars by hanging them from a wire suspended on two posts.

5. To assemble the earrings, take a piece of wire and make a simple loop, then slide it onto the earring before closing the loop. Add a blue seed bead and make another wire loop. Open the wire loop on the ear wire and connect it to this second loop on the earring (see the photo on page 73). Repeat this step to assemble the second earring.

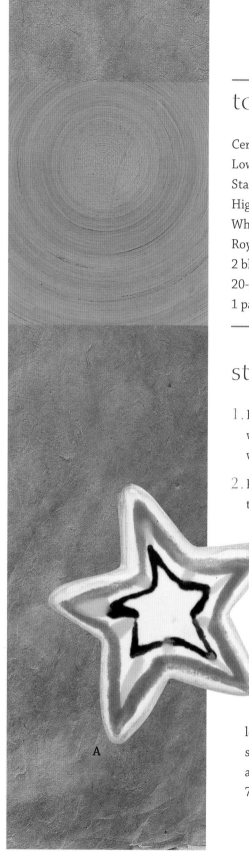

A

raku earrings

Wearing raku ceramic jewelry, like these playful and stylish earrings, is almost as much fun as making it.

A

tools and materials

Ceramic Tool Kit (see page 9)
¼ pound of low-fire white clay
Turquoise raku glaze
Combustible material (such as sawdust)
2 silver head pins, 2 inches (5.1 cm) in length
6 yellow seed beads
2 ear wires

B

step by step

1. Roll a flat piece of clay about ⅛ inch (3 mm) thick. Cut four strips about ¼ x 2 inches (6 mm x 5.1 cm).

2. Attach the ends of two strips together to form a surfboard shape; repeat with the other two strips to form the second bead. Smooth the seams. Pierce a small hole in the top seams on the beads. A head pin will go through this hole, so make it large enough for this purpose.

3. After bisque firing, glaze the beads with the turquoise raku glaze according to the jar's instructions.

4. Load the beads onto a rack that you can easily lift. I made my rack from clay with a loop at the top for easy grabbing.

5. When the kiln reaches temperature, pull the whole rack out of the kiln with tongs and place it into a metal bucket with combustible material like sawdust (see photo A). Carefully cover the rack with more material and close the lid. Let it burn for about a half an hour or until most of the smoke clears.

6. Remove the beads from the combustible material and quench them in water. Use a wire brush to clean off any burnt material remaining on the bead surface (see photo B).

7. To assemble an earring, string three seed beads onto a headpin. String the headpin through the raku bead (see photo C). Make a wire loop and trim the excess wire. Attach the ear wire. Repeat this step to complete the other earring.

something fishy necklace

You don't need
a sculptor's talent
to make this
charmingly shaped
and textured fish.
Periwinkle and
turquoise beads
surround it with
a hint of the sea.

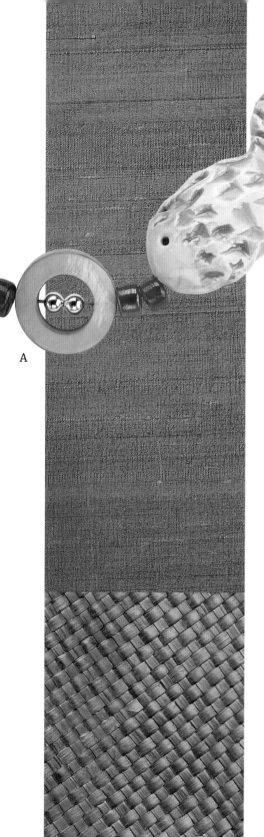

A

tools and materials

Ceramic Tool Kit (see page 9)
Low-fire white clay
Yellow, orange, and brown underglaze
Turquoise and periwinkle glaze
Clear glaze
24 inches (61 cm) of beading wire
Sterling silver clasp
40 pink crow beads
12 lime-green "O" beads, 12 mm in diameter
24 sterling silver beads, 4 mm

step by step

1. Shape a large ball of clay into a rough fish form. After your form has dried a little, use ceramic tools to carve the fish's scales and face. Create a hole lengthwise through the bead (see page 23).

2. Roll out four round balls and two cylinder beads. Texture these beads with stamps, and then bisque-fire all of your beads.

3. Glaze the round beads periwinkle and the cylinder beads turquoise. With orange underglaze, paint a coat over the entire fish. Rub off the glaze with a sponge, leaving glaze in the crevices. Paint yellow underglaze over the high areas, and create the eye with a dot of brown underglaze (see photo A). Clear-glaze your fish and fire all the beads.

4. To string the necklace, start by crimping the bead wire to one end of the toggle, and then continue with the following pattern, as shown in photo B:

- String five pink crow beads and one green "O" bead, with two silver beads strung in the middle of the "O" shape. Whenever you add a green bead, put two silver beads inside it.

- Follow this with four pink crow beads and another green bead.

- Next, string three more crow beads, a green bead, and a periwinkle ball with a crow bead on each side.

- String a green bead, followed by a turquoise cylinder with a crow bead on each side.

- Follow this with another green bead and a periwinkle ball with a crow bead on each side

- String one more green bead and two crow beads.

5. Add your fish bead, and then repeat the pattern, working backwards, on the other side of the necklace. Crimp on the other half of the toggle to complete the necklace (see photo C).

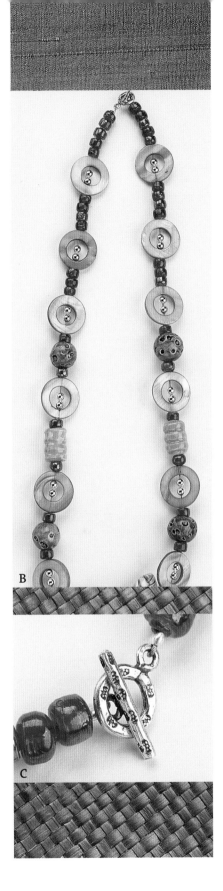

flowery cuff

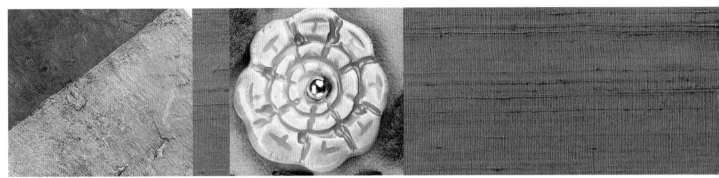

Pretty blooms grow all in a row on this velveteen cuff stitched together with embroidery.

tools and materials

Ceramic Tool Kit (see page 9)
2 medallions or buttons, about 1 inch (2.5 cm) in diameter
Low-fire white clay
5 pastel underglazes
Tan velveteen, 3 x 8-inch (7.6 x 20.3 cm) piece
Green wool felt, 4 x 4-inch (10.2 x 10.2 cm) piece
Brown embroidery floss,1 skein
Needle and thread
5 sterling silver round beads, 4 mm

step by step

1. Make a mold of the two medallions, as described on page 28.

2. Roll some clay into a ball and press it into the mold. Clear away the excess clay and smooth the back. Remove the bead from the mold. If the bead doesn't easily come out of the mold, stick the end of your needle tool into the clay and gently wiggle the bead out. With a skewer, pierce a hole through the center of the bead face. Make a total of five beads.

3. Bisque-fire the beads. Paint each one with a different color of underglaze. Apply a coat of clear glaze to the beads and fire them in the kiln.

4. Fold the velveteen fabric in half with the back of the fabric facing out. Sew one short side and the long side together. Turn the fabric right side out. Fold the rough edges in and sew up the remaining side, carefully hiding your stitches.

5. Lay out the five beads on the fabric, and mark the center of each bead on the fabric with a pencil. Make sure to leave room at one end for the buttonhole, where the cuff will overlap.

6. Cut out four leaf shapes from the felt. Sew these leaves onto the cuff near each pencil mark with the brown embroidery floss. Sew a line of embroidery floss around the edge of the cuff to create a border.

7. With a needle and thread, sew the beads onto the cuff over the leaves. Bring the needle up through the center of the ceramic bead. Run the needle through the sterling silver bead and back through the ceramic bead (see photo A). Attach all five beads in this manner.

8. Cut a slit into the cuff a little smaller than the ceramic bead. Try sliding the bead through the hole; if it doesn't fit, enlarge the hole slightly until it does. Overstitch around the edges of the hole to prevent fraying, this will be your buttonhole (see photo B).

cupid ring

With its swirly red bead mounted in hand-sculpted metal clay, this charming ring will go straight to your heart.

A

B

tools and materials

Ceramic Tool Kit (see page 9)
Low-fire white clay
Red crackle glaze
Texture stamp
Metal clay
Wooden dowel or ring mandrel

step by step

1. Roll out a piece of the low-fire clay to approximately ¼ inch (6 mm) thick. Cut out a heart shape that is 1 inch (2.5 cm) in diameter. Smooth the edges and send a hole through the side of the bead at a slight angle. This is where you will place the arrow.

2. Bisque-fire the bead and glaze it with the red glaze. Do not glaze the back of the bead. If you leave the bead's back porous, the metal clay will adhere better. Fire the bead.

3. Roll out a piece of metal clay. I use playing cards the same way I use wooden slats to roll out a consistent piece of clay. My ring is five cards thick. Cut a ½ x 3-inch (1.3 x 7.6 cm) rectangle for the ring. Smooth the edges and wrap around the mandrel. As you size your ring, remember that metal clay shrinks 10 to 28 percent, depending on the clay. Trim off the excess metal clay and join the two ends together.

4. Roll out a coil of the metal clay. Form the arrowhead at one end and the arrow's feathered end on the other end. Cut the coil in half and insert each end into the holes in the heart bead (see photo A).

5. With another small piece of metal clay, attach the two coils that form the arrow behind the heart bead, then attach the heart bead to the ring (see photo B). Let the piece dry slowly.

6. Fire the entire piece in a bowl of alumina hydrate to the recommended temperature.

7. Let the entire piece cool completely in the kiln before removing. With a wire brush, clean off the fire scale.

piazza necklace

Majolica beads in sun-drenched colors make this necklace the perfect accessory for shopping in a market in Florence—or for going to the pizza place around the corner.

sweet little bee earrings

A   B

Start some buzz about your choice of accessories with these cute black and yellow earrings.

tools and materials

Ceramic Tool Kit (see page 9)
¼ pound of low-fire white clay
Black and yellow underglazes
Clear glaze
2 sterling silver balls, 4 mm
2 opaque lime flower drops, 6 mm
2 sterling silver head pins, 2 inches (5.1 cm) in length
2 flower motif ear wires

step by step

1. Roll two matching ½-inch (1.3 cm) balls. Pierce a hole in each bead. Set them aside to dry.

2. After bisque-firing the beads, use black and yellow underglazes to paint several bees onto the beads with a fine brush. Make the bee bodies with the flat end of a skewer to get a nice round circle. Add stripes and wings with a fine brush and black paint (see photo A).

3. Apply clear glaze to the beads. Suspend the beads on a wire hanging off two stilts. Fire to the recommended temperature.

4. To assemble the earrings, string the silver ball, the flower drop, and bee bead onto a head pin. Using the round nose pliers, make a wire loop above the ceramic bead and slide on the ear wire. Finish the loop and trim the wire (see photo B). Repeat to finish the second earring.

pencil scratch pendant

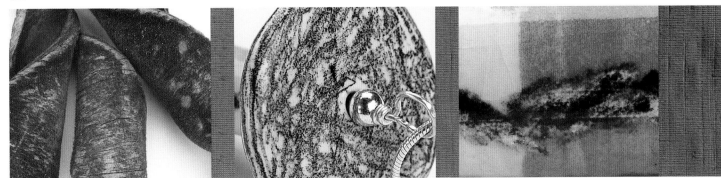

Your choice of decorative techniques with ceramic beads is nearly limitless— as shown here, where simple pencil scratches become art.

tools and materials

Ceramic Tool Kit (see page 9)
¼ pound of low-fire white clay
Underglaze pencil
Red and yellow underglaze
Clear glaze
1 sterling silver ball, 4 mm
1 textured sterling silver ball, 6 mm
20-gauge sterling silver head pin, 5-inch (12.7 cm) in length
16-inch (40.6 cm) sterling silver 1 mm snake chain

step by step

1. Using an extruder with ⅓-inch (8.5 mm) circular opening, extrude a clay tube and cut a 1½-inch (3.8 cm) cylinder. Smooth the two ends and carefully pierce a hole lengthwise through the bead.

2. Make a round bead and flatten it into a circle about 1 inch (2.5 cm) in diameter. Pierce the hole through the center of the circle's face.

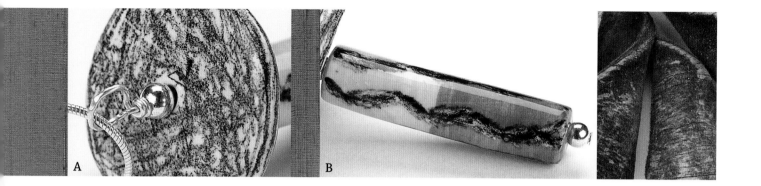

A   B

3. After drying them completely, bisque-fire the beads.

4. To decorate the circle bead, use the underglaze pencil and draw loose lines covering all of its surface (see photo A).

5. Paint half of the tube bead red and half yellow. After the underglaze dries, draw a zigzag design down the sides with the underglaze pencil (see photo B).

6. Apply two coats of clear glaze over the beads, dabbing on the first coat so you don't smear the pencil designs. Fire the beads in the kiln by suspending them on wire between two stilts.

7. To assemble the pendant, string a 4 mm silver ball onto the headpin, followed by the tube bead, a 6 mm silver ball, and the circle bead.

8. Finish the head pin with a basic wire loop (see page 48). Make sure the loop is large enough to accommodate the end of the snake chain. String the pendant onto the chain.

square bead bracelet

Get as creative as you want with the designs and symbols you carve into these multicolor beads.

tools and materials

Ceramic Tool Kit (see page 9)
Low-fire white clay
Pink, yellow, lime, turquoise, and black underglazes
Fine sandpaper (optional)
8 matte black round glass beads, 8 mm
Sterling silver toggle clasp

step by step

1. Roll out a coil of clay about 8 inches (20.3 cm) long and 1 inch (2.5 cm) thick. Using a ruler as a guide, cut about ten pieces of clay to the same size. I cut mine every ½ inch (1.3 cm).

2. Make ten flat, square beads out of the cut pieces, as shown on page 26. An average-sized bracelet will need seven beads, but make extra, so you can size it perfectly and so you can pick your favorite beads.

3. While the beads are still wet, carefully place them on skewers. Paint the beads with the colored underglazes, overlapping layers of color. Let the beads dry to a leather-hard state.

A

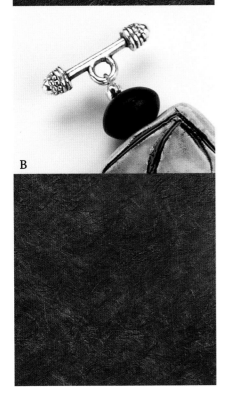

B

4. With a sharp ceramic tool, carve into the beads, making designs on both sides of all seven beads. Let the beads dry completely on the skewers.

5. After the beads have dried completely, carefully remove them from the skewers. Clean off any rough spots with a sharp tool or fine sandpaper. When they're ready, bisque-fire them.

6. Paint a layer of black underglaze over the beads, making sure to get it into all the cracks and crevices. Wipe the black underglaze off of the beads, but leave it in the crevices. Paint on two coats of clear glaze and fire a second time.

7. To assemble the bracelet, lay out seven of the beads placing a black glass bead between each one (see photo A). Measure to see if this is the correct size for your wrist. You might need to add or subtract beads to get the right length. Once you've got the bracelet arranged the way you would like it, crimp half of the toggle onto the beading wire. String the beads onto it in the order you laid them out and finish by crimping the remaining side of the toggle onto the wire (see photo B).

spiral ring

Twisting wire surrounds a polka-dot flat bead and a silver ball, holding everything in place with a flourish.

tools and materials

Ceramic Tool Kit (see page 9)
Low-fire white clay
1-inch (2.5 cm) circle cutter
Yellow and orange underglaze
Clear glaze
Silver pillow disc bead
20-gauge sterling silver wire, 40 inches (101.6 cm) in length

step by step

1. Roll out a piece of clay to ⅛ inch (3 mm) width. With the circle cutter, make a disc. Round the edges of the bead with your fingers. Pierce a hole through the center of the bead's face. Let the bead dry completely and then bisque-fire it.

2. Paint a coat of yellow underglaze on the bead. Using the end of a skewer and the orange glaze, cover all sides of the bead with orange polka dots. Apply clear glaze to the bead, and fire to the recommended temperature.

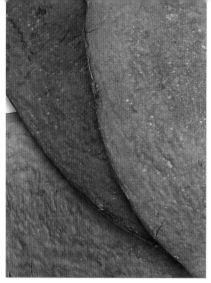

A

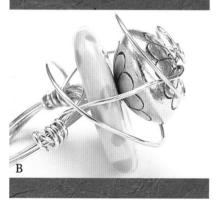

B

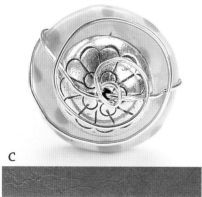

C

3. Cut a 20-inch (50.8 cm) piece of wire and wrap it three times around a dowel rod or marker to make a circle shape, leaving 4 inches (10.2 cm) of straight wire at each end. Adjust the wire's circumference to get the desired size of ring.

4. With another 20-inch (50.8 cm) length of wire, wrap a few turns around one side of the wire ring you made in step 3 (see photo A).

5. Form the loose end of the wrapping wire along the top of the ring, and align all three wire ends in the middle of the ring. Bend the wires as necessary so they're grouped snugly together.

6. Slide the ceramic and metal bead onto the three wires. Bend two of the wires along the sides of the beads then secure the ends by wrapping them around the sides of the ring a few times, as shown in photo B. Trim the excess wire.

7. Twist the remaining wire where it comes out of the bead with the needle-nose pliers. Fashion it into a spiral from the top of the ring over to the side in only one wrap (see photo C). Wrap it securely around the ring and trim the excess wire.

polka dot fun bracelet

The subtle curve you give to the large square bead
in this bracelet adds both comfort and style.

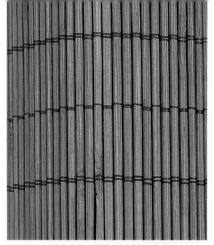

tools and materials

Ceramic Tool Kit (see page 9)
Low-fire white clay
Black underglaze
Clear matte glaze
¾-inch (1.9 cm) black ribbon, 8 inches (20.3 cm) in length
1 set of ¾-inch (1.9 cm) ribbon terminators
Sterling silver ball clasp

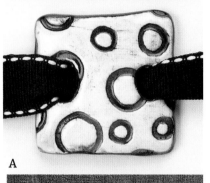

A

B

step by step

1. Roll out a piece of clay ⅙ inch (4.2 mm) thick. With a 2-inch (5.1 cm) square cookie cutter, cut out one square. Cut two circles out of the square, each measuring ½ inch (1.3 cm) in diameter, near opposite edges (see photo A). Smooth all the edges and stamp a design into the front of the bead (see photo A again).

2. Gently curve the bead and let it dry draped over a curved form such as a cardboard tube.

3. After bisque-firing, paint a coat of black underglaze on the bead. With a sponge, wipe off the front of the bead, leaving the black underglaze only in the crevices.

4. Apply two or three coats of the clear matte glaze. Fire to the recommended temperature.

5. Weave the ribbon through the holes in the bead (see photo B). Attach the ribbon terminators to the ribbon, and then attach one half of the clasp to one terminator and the other half to the second terminator.

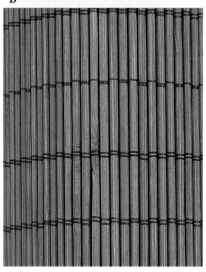

tree in a
forest necklace

*Go natural with these green ceramic leaves entwined
in brown and green silk and hemp.*

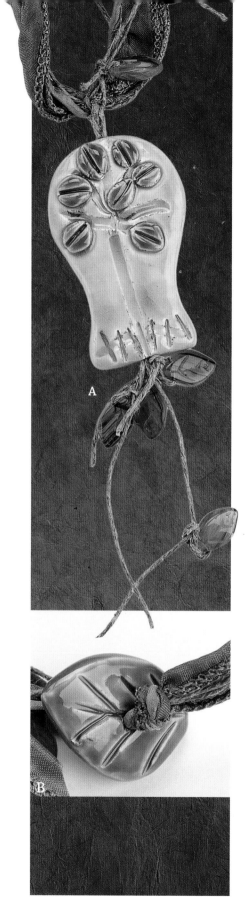

tools and materials

Ceramic Tool Kit (see page 9)
Low-fire white clay
Olive green and ochre glazes
1 spool natural hemp
16 green glass leaves, 6 mm
Green silk cord, 27 inches (68.6 cm) in length
Brown silk ribbon, 27 inches (68.6 cm) in length

step by step

1. Roll out a piece of clay ¼ inch (6 mm) thick. With the needle tool, cut out a tree shape for the pendant (see photo A) and a leaf shape for the closure (see photo B). Smooth the edges.

2. Carve veins into the leaf bead with the needle tool. Push a hole through the center of the leaf shape.

3. Hand-form seven smaller leaf shapes from clay. Score the backs and attach them to the pendant by pressing firmly. Carve a vein down the center of each leaf with the needle tool.

4. With a skewer, create the other lines for the tree bead. Pierce a hole through the length of the bead. After the bisque firing, glaze the leaves green and the background ochre.

5. Glaze-fire all the beads.

6. To assemble the necklace, cut four pieces of the hemp about 40 inches (101.6 cm) long. Tie one glass leaf bead on each strand near the end. Tie all four of the strands together with a half knot. Thread all four lengths of hemp through the focal bead.

7. Fold the silk cord and ribbon in half and tie the hemp around the center point. Tie the remaining glass leaf beads onto the hemp spacing them sporadically along the strands.

8. Slide the leaf bead on one end of the necklace and tie a half knot with all four strands. With the strands on the opposite side, make a loop just a little larger than the leaf. Tie a knot and trim the excess strands close to the knot.

blooming pendant

Shimmering silver luster outlines the blooms and leaves stamped into this pendant. Delicate silk cords tie it all together.

A

B

tools and materials

Ceramic Tool Kit (see page 9)
Low-fire white clay
High-temperature wire
Purple underglaze
Black underglaze stamp pad
Rubber stamp with floral design
Clear glaze
Silver luster
4 coordinating silk cords, each 40 inches (101.6 cm) in length

step by step

1. Roll out a flat piece of clay about ⅛ inch (3 mm) thick. With a cookie cutter or the needle tool, cut out an oval shape. The oval I made measured 2 x 3 inches (5.1 x 7.6 cm). Smooth the edges with your fingers. Make two small wire loops from the high-temperature wire (see page 24). Add the loops to the top edge of the pendant so it hangs properly when worn. Place the pendant between plaster boards to dry.

2. After bisque firing, brush on a light coat of purple underglaze. (I added water to the glaze to give it a watercolor effect.) Then use the rubber stamp to press a design of black underglaze onto the pendant (see photo A). After the ink has dried completely, apply clear glaze to the pendant and fire it.

3. Paint luster accents onto the pendant with a detail brush (see photo B). Let the luster dry overnight. Place the pendant back into the kiln for a third firing. The piece can lie on its back, as long as the luster is only on the front. Leave the kiln lid cracked open during the firing to let the gases escape.

4. Slide the four silk strands through one loop on the pendant, and tie a knot. Slide the strands through the other loop, pull them snug, and tie another knot. To wear the necklace, simply tie the ends in a bow.

autumn bounty necklace

Harvest time is here. Ceramic leaves, buckeyes, and acorns dance merrily on a fall-hued necklace.

tools and materials

Ceramic Tool Kit (see page 9)
Red earthenware clay
Gold, brown, light green, and dark green glazes
Beading wire
Crimps
30 inches (76.2 cm) of red agate chips, laid in a row
20 copper coil beads, each 1 inch (2.5 cm) in length
30 inches (76.2 cm) of copper chain
10 round copper beads, 2 mm
10 copper head pins
Red agate toggle

step by step

1. Make an acorn-shaped bead by first rolling a ball of clay into a cone shape. Next, make a flat circle bead as described on page 26. Push the flat circle on top of the cone. Now you have a rough acorn shape. With your fingers and tools, shape the bead into a proper acorn (see photo A). Put a hole through the bead lengthwise. I added texture on the cap of the bead with the end of a skewer. Make nine more acorn beads.

2. Make a buckeye-shaped bead by rolling out a ball and pressing a pencil eraser into one side of it (see photo B). Pierce the bead crosswise with a hole. Make six more.

A

B

C

D

3. Next, roll out a thin piece of clay. Cut out 20 leaf shapes with a needle tool and then smooth the edges. I pressed leaves from my yard into the clay to give the beads leaf textures and veins (see photo C). With a skewer, put a hole through the top of the clay leaves.

4. Bisque-fire all the beads. Glaze the leaves several different colors of green and brown. Glaze the acorns with brown and gold.

5. The necklace has three strands that connect in the back with an agate toggle. The first strand is agate and buckeyes strung on beading wire. Connect one end of the beading wire with a crimp and then string the agate, spacing the buckeyes evenly throughout. Finish by crimping the end to the second side of the toggle.

6. The second strand has copper coils and leaves. String this strand by alternating coils and leaves until the length is the same length as the first strand. Connect both ends to the toggle, as you did for the first strand.

7. The third strand is composed of acorns and copper chain. First, measure and cut a chain to the same length as the previous two strands. Lay out the chain in a straight line. String a copper ball and an acorn onto each head pin. With a wire loop, connect each head pin to the chain. Once you've attached all the acorns, connect the ends of the copper chain to the toggle (see photo D).

metal and clay pendant

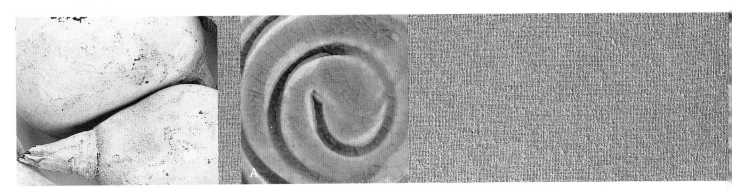

A

Pairing metal clay with low-fired clay can yield dramatic results.

tools and materials

Ceramic Tool Kit (see page 9)
Low-fire white clay
Spiral stamp
High-temperature wire
Seafoam green glaze
Sand glaze
Metal clay
Brown leather cording, 22 inches (55.9 cm)
Sterling silver clasp

step by step

1. Roll out a thin piece of clay approximately ⅛ inch (3 mm) thick. Cut out the trapezoid shape for the charm that will hang from the tube bead. Smooth the edges and stamp your spiral stamp into the clay (see photo A). Make a loop of high-temperature wire and insert it into the charm's top side.

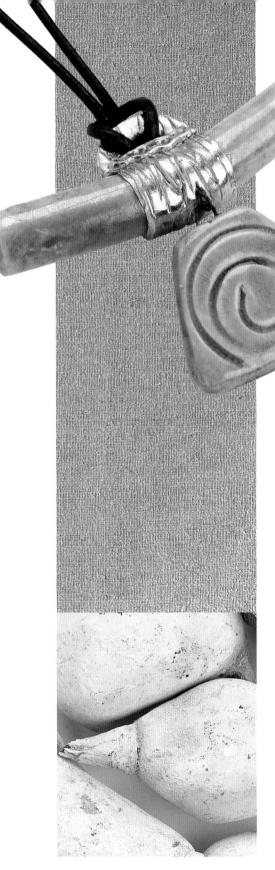

2. Next, extrude a tube of clay measuring ¼ x 2 inches (3 mm x 5.1 cm). Smooth the ends and pierce a hole through the bead, as explained on page 23. The metal clay will hide this hole later in the process.

3. Thread wire through the loop of the trapezoid charm. Make a loop with the wire and then insert it into the tube.

4. After bisque-firing, glaze the charm with the green glaze and the tube with the sand glaze. Clean all the glaze off the wire loops. Insert a temporary wire through the hole in the tube to hang the pendant, and then fire the pieces.

5. Roll out a piece of metal clay as thin as you can get it. Cut out a rectangle ½ inch (1.3 cm) by the circumference of the tube bead, adding another ½ inch (1.3 cm) to the length. Round the corners of one end of the rectangle. Cut out a half circle at that end, following the curve you just made, for the leather cord to slide through. Then cut a slit halfway up the rectangle.

6. Wrap the metal clay around the tube bead. With a small skewer, push the straight end of the metal clay into the rounded end. Make four indents across the seam with the end of the skewer. Turn the skewer around and use the point to carve lines into the metal clay.

7. Let the metal clay dry completely. If there are any rough edges, sand them with a nail file. Lay the pendant in a bowl of sodium silicate or place it directly onto a kiln shelf. Fire to the recommended temperature on the package of your metal clay.

8. When you take the pendant out of the kiln, the metal will be white. Apply a brass wire brush to the metal until it shines.

9. To assemble the pendant, fold the leather in half. Pass the fold through the hole in the pendant. Send the two loose ends around and through the loop. Pull the leather snug. Tie each end of leather to a clasp with a simple knot or crimp the leather inside the clasp ends, depending on the type of clasp you have.

raku focal pendant

Raku is a centuries-old technique from Japan. The earthy tones of the central disk, combined with turquoise and silver, give this pendant more of a Southwestern feeling.

tools and materials

Ceramic Tool Kit (see page 9)
Low-fire white clay
Two circular stamps, for the pendant and the flat circle beads
High-temperature wire
Crusty matte raku glaze
Turquoise, red, and orange raku glaze
4 crimp beads, 2 mm in diameter
40 inches (101.6 cm) of beading wire
12 faceted tourmaline stones
18 sterling silver spacers
16 red agate stones
Sterling silver toggle

step by step

1. Roll out a flat piece of clay until it is about 1/8 inch (3 mm) thick. Cut out a disk that measures 2½ inches (6.4 cm) in diameter, and then stamp a circle into the center of the shape.

2. Use a thin, straight object, such as a skewer, to create lines radiating from the circle to the edge of the pendant. Insert two wire loops into the side of the pendant about 1½ inches (3.8 cm) apart; see photo A for positioning. Then let it dry between two plaster boards.

3. Next, make six ball beads approximately ½ inch (1.3 cm) in diameter and set these aside to dry. Roll out two flat circle beads with a small, round stamp in the center. Also make two long cylinder beads that taper at the ends, and use the small round stamp to cover it with dots. Bisque-fire all of your beads.

4. Glaze the pendant border, the long tubes, and the flat circle beads using the crusty matte raku glaze. Use the turquoise raku glaze for the pendant's center and for the six small ball beads. Glaze the dots on the long tubes using the red raku glaze (see photo B). Glaze the center of the flat circle beads using the orange raku glaze. Fire all the beads following the raku instructions on page 46.

B

C

D

5. To assemble the necklace, begin by crimping a piece of beading wire to the focal pendant. String beads onto the wire following this pattern:

- String a tourmaline bead, a spacer bead, a ceramic ball, a spacer, an agate, and another spacer. Next, string on one of the long cylinder beads and two red agates with silver spacers on each side (see photo C, moving from the bottom up).

- Follow these with a ceramic ball, a spacer, a tourmaline, a flat circle, and another tourmaline (see photo D, moving from the bottom up).

- String, two agates, and a ceramic ball with silver spacers on each side.

- Next, string a tourmaline bead with two agates on each side.

- Finish up by stringing two silver spacers, two agates, a tourmaline, two more agates, and a tourmaline.

6. Crimp the wire to one side of the clasp. String the second side of the necklace using the same pattern.

charming bag charm

*Why limit yourself
to self-adornment?
Beads can serve
as delightful
embellishments
for bags, key rings,
and bookmarks.*

tools and materials

Ceramic Tool Kit (see page 9)
Low-fire white clay
High-temperature wire
Blue and brown glaze
5 glass tiger striped beads
6 gold glass beads
3 silver diamond beads
3 decorative head pins
20-gauge sterling silver wire, 3 inches (7.6 cm) in length
1 large bag or lanyard clip

step by step

1. Roll out a piece of clay about ⅛ inch (3 mm) thick. With a needle tool, cut
   out a 2-inch (5.1 cm) square. In the middle of that square, cut out a 1-inch
   (2.5 cm) square. Smooth the edges. Make four small wire loops with the
   high-temperature wire (see page 24), and add one of the wire loops at the
   top center edge of the square. Insert the other three wire loops spaced
   evenly across the bottom (see photo A).

B

2. Bisque-fire the charm. Glaze the top half of the charm (the area with the single loop) with the blue glaze. Glaze the bottom half with the brown glaze. Overlap the two glazes where they meet, which will force the two glazes to combine and run together.

3. Hang the charm on a wire in the kiln. Make sure you hang the charm from the top loop so the glazes run down.

4. To assemble the bag charm, make a simple wire loop and connect it to the clip. String a tiger glass bead onto the wire and make another loop, and connect it to the charm.

5. To string the head pins, begin with one of the outside two loops on the bottom of the charm. Start with a gold bead, then string a tiger bead, and finally, string a silver diamond. Make a wire loop on the head pin above the beads and connect it to the charm (see page 48). Repeat this for the head pin on the other outside loop on the bottom of the charm.

6. String the last head pin with a gold bead, a tiger bead, another gold bead, a diamond bead, a third gold bead, another tiger bead, and one last gold bead (see photo B). Make a wire loop on the head pin above the strung beads and attach it to the middle loop on the bottom of the charm.

tropical colors
charm bracelet

Beach chair, fruity drink, sandy white beach, azure water—
this island bracelet could be the spark for a dream vacation
(or, at least, a beautiful daydream).

A

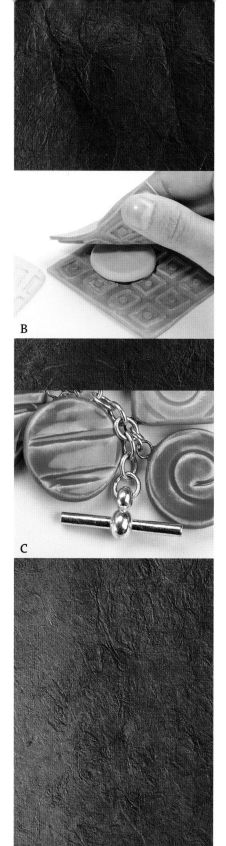

B

C

tools and materials

Ceramic Tool Kit (see page 9)
¼ pound of low-fire white clay
Variety of small stamps
High-temperature wire
Lime, orange, and turquoise glazes
Link bracelet for the charms
20 sterling silver 3 mm jump rings

step by step

1. Make 21 shape charms, forming circles, triangles, and squares. Stamp both sides of the beads with assorted designs (see photo A). To keep the same depth of the impression on both sides, press a stamp into each side of the bead simultaneously (see photo B).

2. With the round-nose pliers, create small loops of high-temperature wire for each bead. Insert one loop into each bead. Let the beads dry completely.

3. After bisque-firing, divide the beads into three groups of seven. Glaze each group of beads a different color. Each bead will need three coats of the colored glaze. Let each coat dry before applying the next.

4. Hang the beads off wires inserted into a fire brick. Glaze fire the charms to the recommended temperature.

5. Lay out the link bracelet on your work surface. Evenly distribute the charms along the bracelet, leaving a few open links on the bracelet by the toggle bar (see photo C).

6. Attach the charms by opening the jump rings with the flat-nose pliers. Slide the ring onto the link bracelet and through the wire loop of the bead.

pearl bail necklace

Diluting underglazes produces a watercolor effect. Here, a pearl-like bead serves as the focus of a necklace with an Asian look.

tools and materials

Ceramic Tool Kit (see page 9)
Low-fire white clay
¾-inch (1.9 cm) dowel rod
Lavender, yellow, brown, and green underglazes
Clear overglaze
Beading wire
Crimps
Lobster claw clasp
3 strands of earth-tone pearls, each 20 inches (50.8 cm) in length
1 strand of wooden round beads, 20 inches (50.8 cm) in length

step by step

1. Roll out a piece of clay ⅛ inch (3 mm) thick. Cut a strip 2½ inches (6.4 cm) wide. Roll the strip of clay around the dowel rod. Trim the clay where the two pieces meet and join them. Smooth the edges and seam and let the clay dry until it sets. Slide the bail off the dowel and let it dry completely. Bisque-fire the piece.

2. With the lavender underglaze watered down, paint flower petals all around the bail. Paint a second coat, this time with of regular-strength lavender, around some of the bail's edges. Paint yellow centers on the flowers, with brown dots. Paint the side edges of the bail brown. With the green, paint some leaves and vines around the bail (see photo A). Cover the outside of the bail with clear glaze and fire.

3. Cut four pieces of beading wire, each 24 inches (61 cm) in length. With a crimp, attach them all to one end of the lobster claw clasp. String three strands of the wire with the earth-tone pearls and attach the wires to the remaining side of the clasp. String the last strand with the wooden beads (see photo B). Attach this last strand to the remaining side of the clasp.

4. Slide the bail onto the four strands of beads. Hook the claps and then slide the bail over the clasp to hide it.

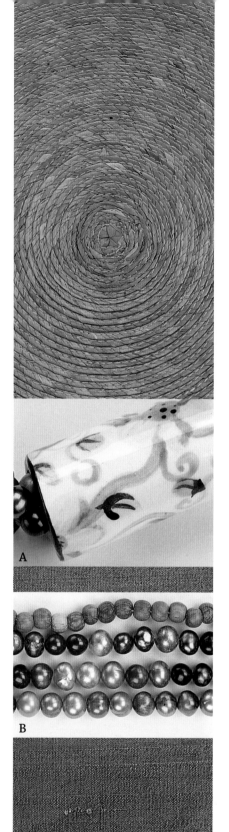

A

B

seed bead pendant

A celebration of color, this necklace combines strands of bold seed beads with a focal pendant that could lead a parade.

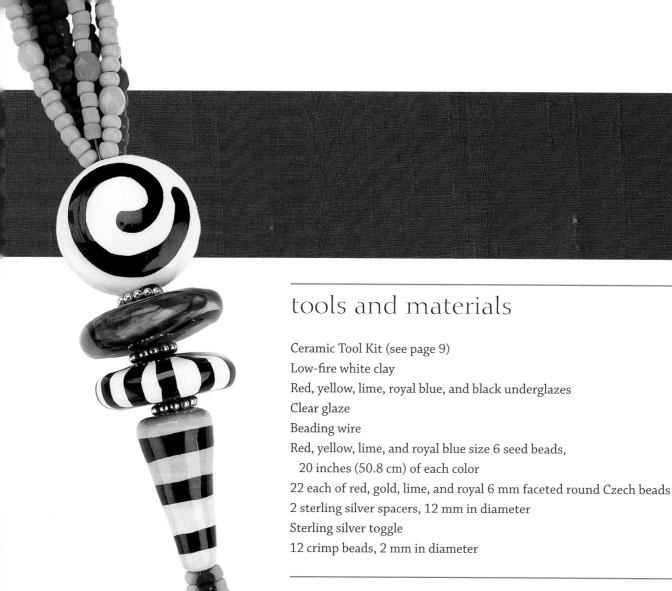

A

tools and materials

Ceramic Tool Kit (see page 9)
Low-fire white clay
Red, yellow, lime, royal blue, and black underglazes
Clear glaze
Beading wire
Red, yellow, lime, and royal blue size 6 seed beads,
 20 inches (50.8 cm) of each color
22 each of red, gold, lime, and royal 6 mm faceted round Czech beads
2 sterling silver spacers, 12 mm in diameter
Sterling silver toggle
12 crimp beads, 2 mm in diameter

step by step

1. Make three flat circle beads measuring about 1¼ inches (3.2 cm) in diameter.
   Pierce a hole going from top to bottom in one bead. Pierce a hole through the
   face of the other two.

2. Roll out a cone bead that measures about 2 inches (5.1 cm) in height.

3. After bisque-firing all the beads, paint a spiral on the circle bead with the hole
   going from top to bottom. Paint black stripes on another, and paint the last
   circle royal blue with red dots. Paint the cone half yellow and half lime. After
   the cone bead has dried, paint stripes around it (see photo A). Coat all the
   beads with clear glaze, and then fire.

B

4. To assemble the necklace, cut four 60-inch (152.4 cm) lengths of beading wire. Find the center of the wire and string on a red bead. Keeping the red bead in place, add one crimp bead on both ends of the wire at the same time and crimp it in place. String seven more seed beads onto both wire ends (see photo B). Repeat this step to add seed beads of a different color to each of the remaining three beading wires.

5. Stick all eight wire ends through the bottom of the cone bead. Add a silver spacer, a flat circle bead, another spacer, the second flat circle bead, and then the upright circle bead.

6. Split the beading wires so that there are four on each side of the necklace. String seed beads onto one wire at a time. After eight seed beads, string a coordinating Czech bead. Continue until you reach the end of the wire. Repeat this step for the other seven wire strands. Each side of the necklace should have one strand of a different color.

7. Crimp the ends of the wires to the toggle.

heart box

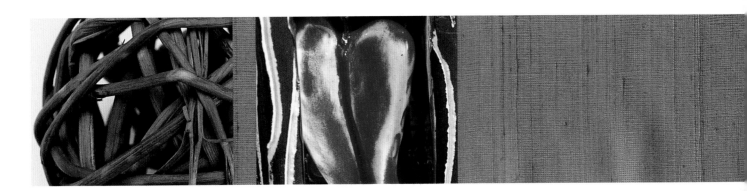

Don't wear your heart on your sleeve. Nestle it safely inside this box-shaped pendant.

tools and materials

Ceramic Tool Kit (see page 9)
Low-fire white clay
High-temperature wire
Clear overglaze
Black, red, light green, and dark green underglazes
Gold luster
2 sterling silver balls, 6 mm
Leather cord, 46 inches (116.8 cm) in length
1 sterling silver hook clasp

step by step

1. To make the box, roll out a piece of clay ⅛ inch (3 mm) thick. Cut out the following pieces: a 2 x 1-inch (5.1 x 2.5 cm) rectangle, two 2 x ⅜-inch (5.1 x 1 cm) rectangles, and two ¾ x ⅜-inch (1.9 x 1 cm) rectangles. Score the edges, add a small amount of slip or water, and join the walls to form a box. Smooth all the seams. About ¼ inch (6 mm) down the side of the box, insert a hole with a skewer. Push the skewer through the opposite wall. Smooth the edges of the holes. Let the box dry to a leather-hard state.

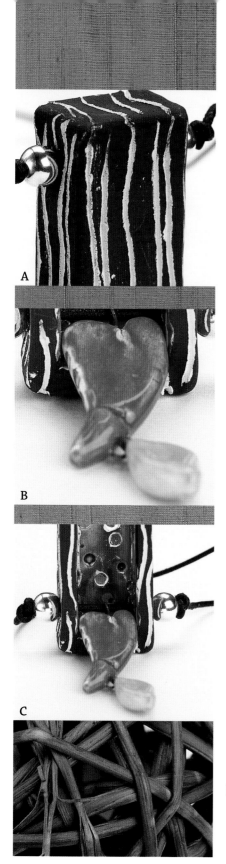

A

B

C

2. While the box is leather-hard, paint a coat of black underglaze over the entire piece. Let the underglaze dry until it does not stick to your fingers when you touch it. Carve curvy stripes into the box with a ceramic tool (see photo A). I like to use a tool that looks like a pointed craft knife. Set the box aside to dry.

3. With a lump of clay, form a small heart and small leaf. Make sure they fit comfortably inside the box together.

4. Carve a line down the center of the heart. With the high-temperature wire, make a wire loop and attach it to the top of the heart so the leather cord can pass through. Attach another small wire loop to the bottom of the heart.

5. Make a small wire loop for the top of the leaf. Before inserting it into the bead, slide it through the loop on the bottom of the heart as shown in photo B. Carefully set both pieces aside to dry.

6. Bisque-fire the two beads. Paint two coats of clear glaze on the inside of the box.

7. Paint the heart with the red underglaze. This is a great time to use hemostats if you have a pair. With a sponge, wipe off the edges of the heart to make it look worn. Paint the leaf light green, and with a shade of darker green, paint veins. Apply two coats of clear glaze to both pieces.

8. Hang the heart bead off a suspended wire with an S-hook. The box can be set directly onto the kiln shelf as it does not have clear glaze on the outside. After the glaze firing, paint two coats of luster inside the box, on top of the clear glaze. Let the luster dry overnight. Fire to the recommended temperature, leaving the kiln lid cracked ¼ inch (6 mm) to allow gases to escape.

9. To assemble the necklace, tie a knot near the middle of the leather cord. On the "long" side, string a silver ball onto the cord, followed by one side of the box. String the heart bead onto the cord, and then continue through the remaining side of the box (see photo C). Follow with the second silver ball. Add a knot to the cord snug against the silver ball.

10. Trim the leather cord to the desired length, leaving equal amounts on each side. Tie the hook clasp onto one end with a knot. Make a loop and tie a knot on the other side of the necklace.